FOR ORGANS, PIANOS & ELECTRONIC KEYBOARDS

E Z PLAY TODAY

103

TWO-CHORD SONGS

ISBN 978-1-4803-4208-8

7777 W. BLUEMOUND RD. P.O. BOX 13819 MILWAUKEE, WI 53213

E-Z Play® Today Music Notation © 1975 by HAL LEONARD CORPORATION
E-Z PLAY and EASY ELECTRONIC KEYBOARD MUSIC are registered trademarks of HAL LEONARD CORPORATION

ABC

Registration 9
Rhythm: Rock

Words and Music by Alphonso Mizell,
Frederick Perren, Deke Richards and Berry Gordy

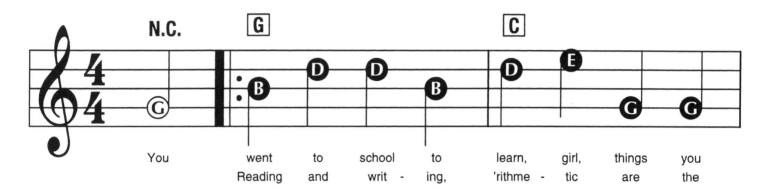

You / Reading
went / and
to / writ -
school / ing,
to / 'rithme -
learn, girl, / tic
things / are
you / the

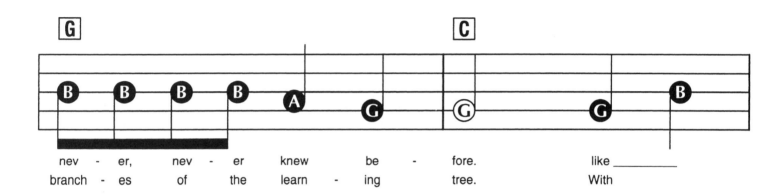

nev - er, / branch - es
nev - er / of
knew / the
be - / learn -
fore. / ing
/ tree.
like _____ / With

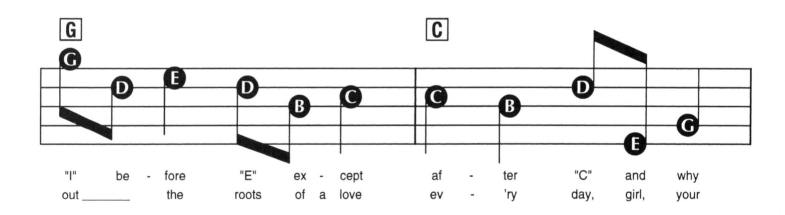

"I" / out _____
be - fore / the
"E" / roots
ex - cept / of a love
af - / ev -
ter / 'ry
"C" / day, girl,
and / why
why / your

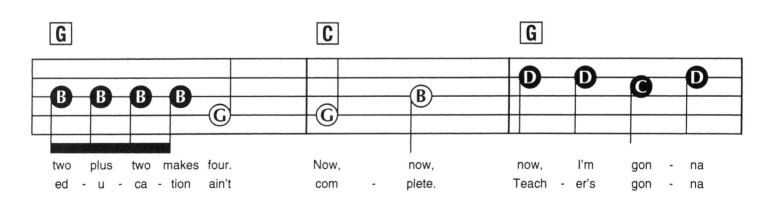

two / ed -
plus / u -
two / ca -
makes / tion
four. / ain't
Now, / com -
now, / plete.
now, I'm / Teach - er's
gon - na / gon - na

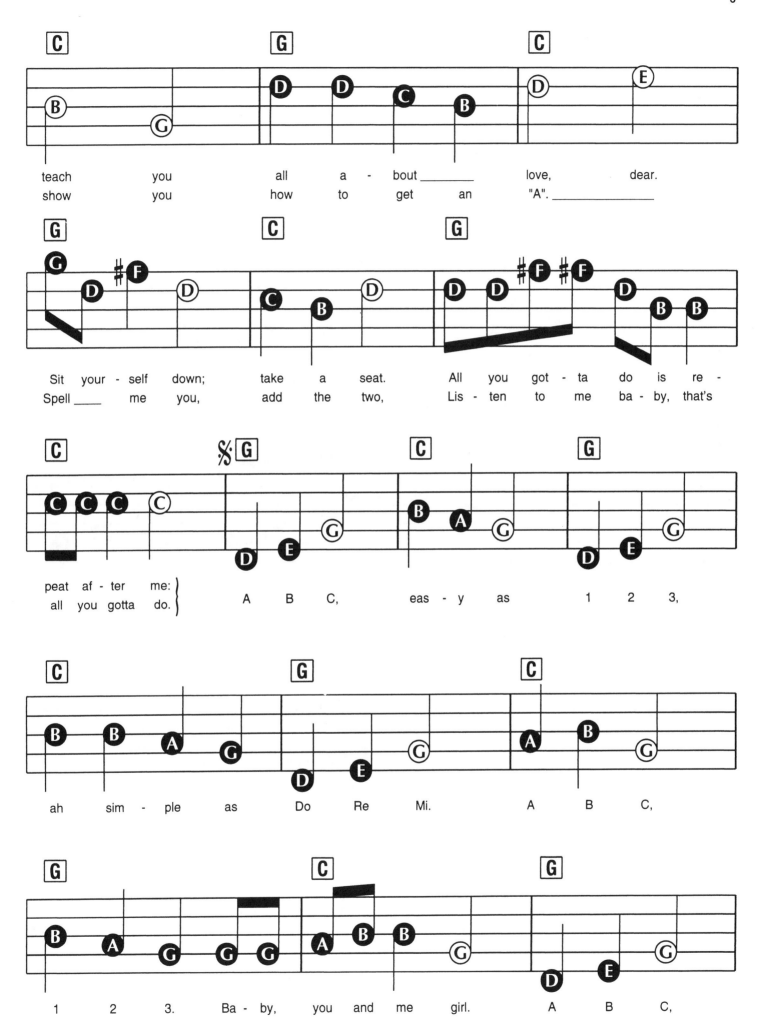

4

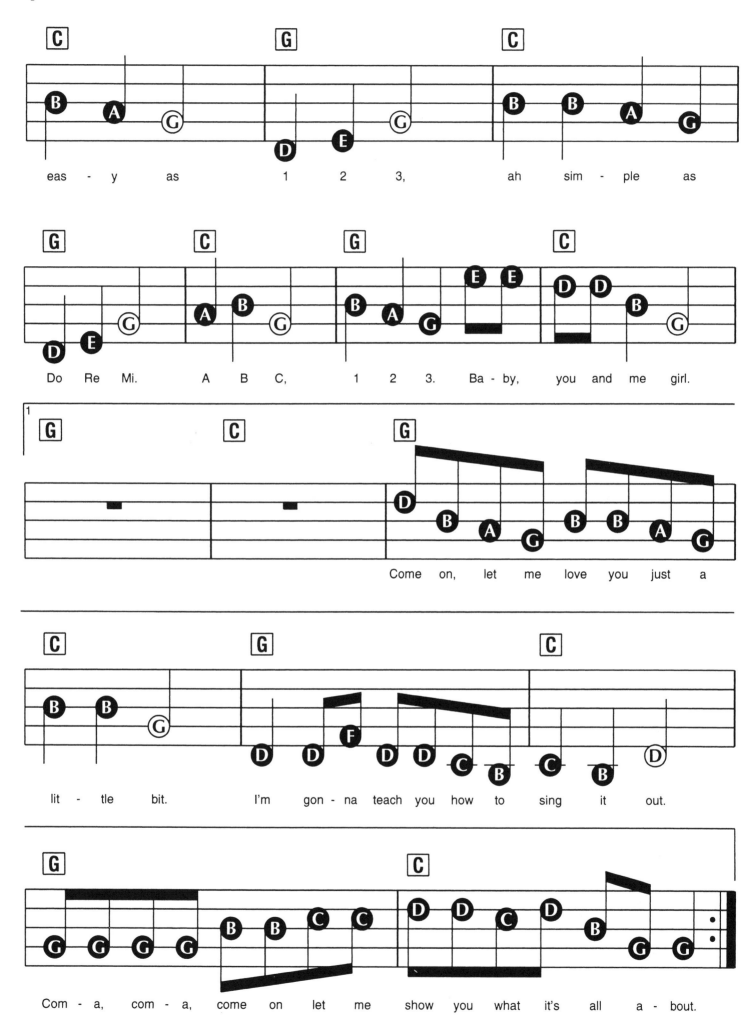

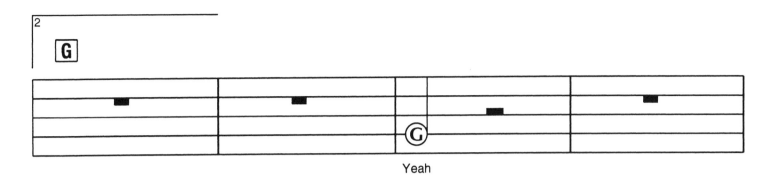

Yeah

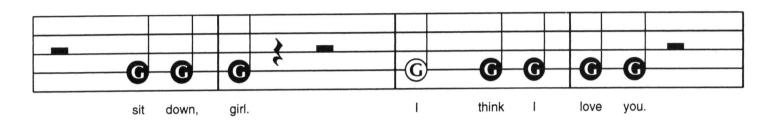

sit down, girl. I think I love you.

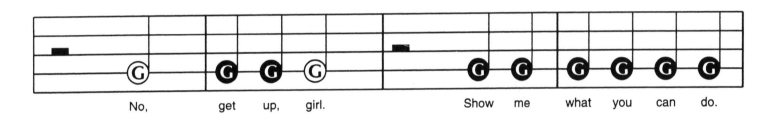

No, get up, girl. Show me what you can do.

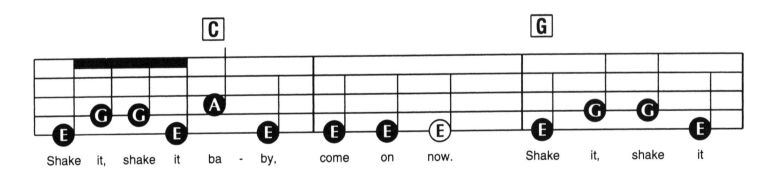

Shake it, shake it ba - by, come on now. Shake it, shake it

D.S. and Fade
(Return to 𝄋
and Fade)

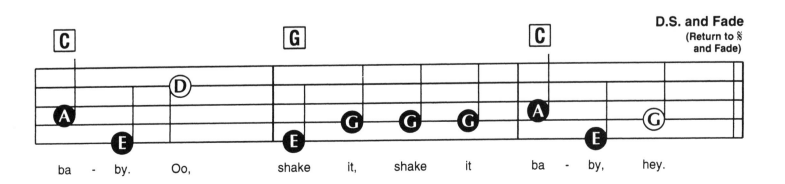

ba - by. Oo, shake it, shake it ba - by, hey.

Achy Breaky Heart
(Don't Tell My Heart)

Registration 5
Rhythm: Rock or 8-Beat

Words and Music by
Don Von Tress

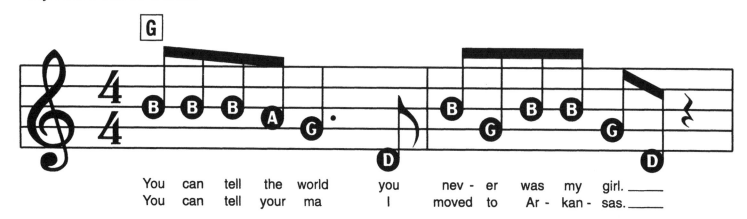

You can tell the world   you   nev - er was my girl. _____
You can tell your ma   I   moved to Ar - kan - sas. _____

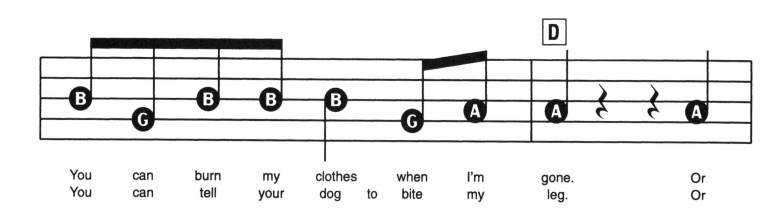

You   can   burn   my   clothes   when   I'm   gone.   Or
You   can   tell   your   dog   to   bite   my   leg.   Or

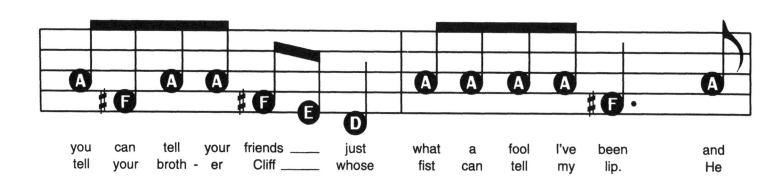

you can tell your friends _____ just   what a fool I've been   and
tell your broth - er Cliff _____ whose   fist can tell my lip.   He

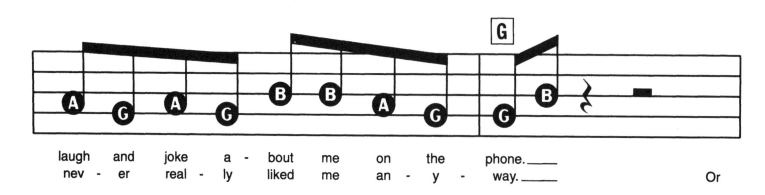

laugh and joke a - bout me on the phone. _____
nev - er real - ly liked me an - y - way. _____   Or

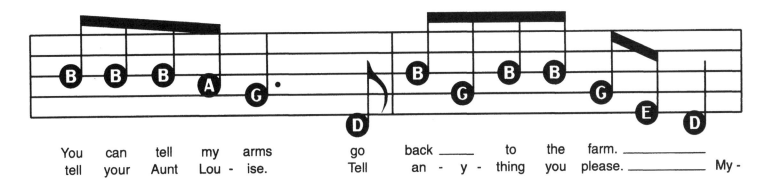

You can tell my arms go back ___ to the farm. ___
tell your Aunt Lou - ise. Tell an - y - thing you please. ___ My -

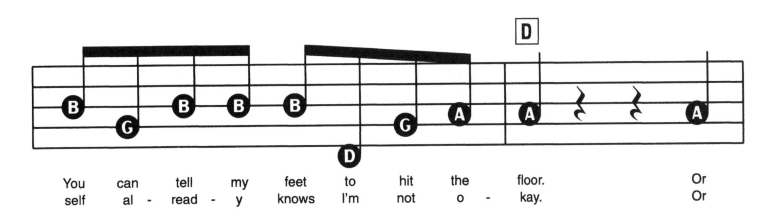

You can tell my feet to hit the floor. Or
self al - read - y knows I'm not o - kay. Or

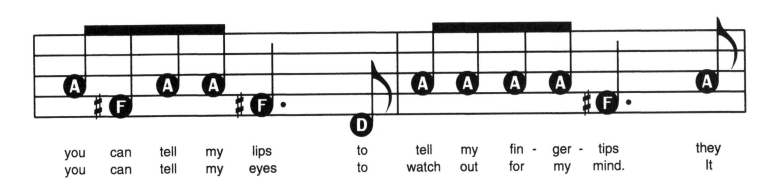

you can tell my lips to tell my fin - ger - tips they
you can tell my eyes to watch out for my mind. It

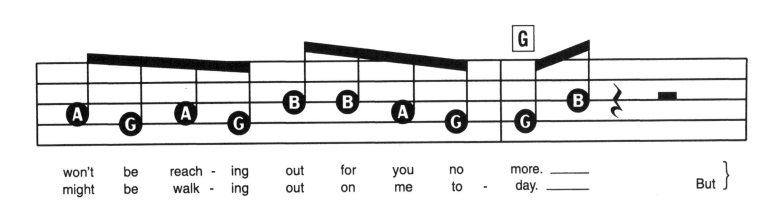

won't be reach - ing out for you no more. ___
might be walk - ing out on me to - day. ___ But

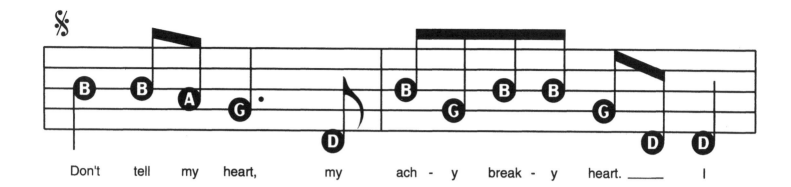

Don't tell my heart, my ach - y break - y heart. _____ I

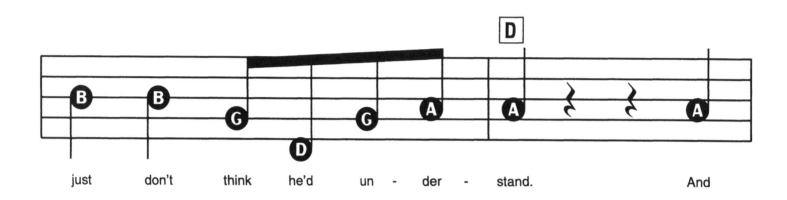

just don't think he'd un - der - stand. And

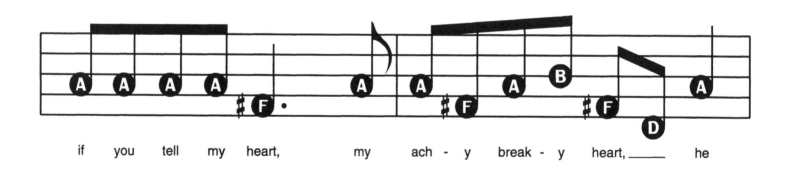

if you tell my heart, my ach - y break - y heart, _____ he

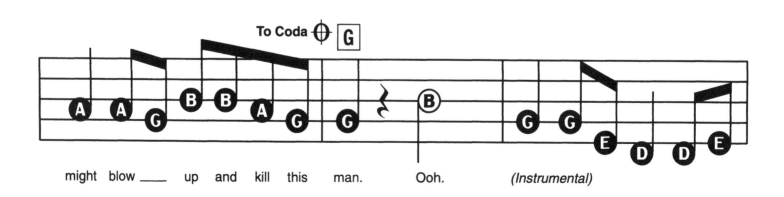

might blow _____ up and kill this man. Ooh. *(Instrumental)*

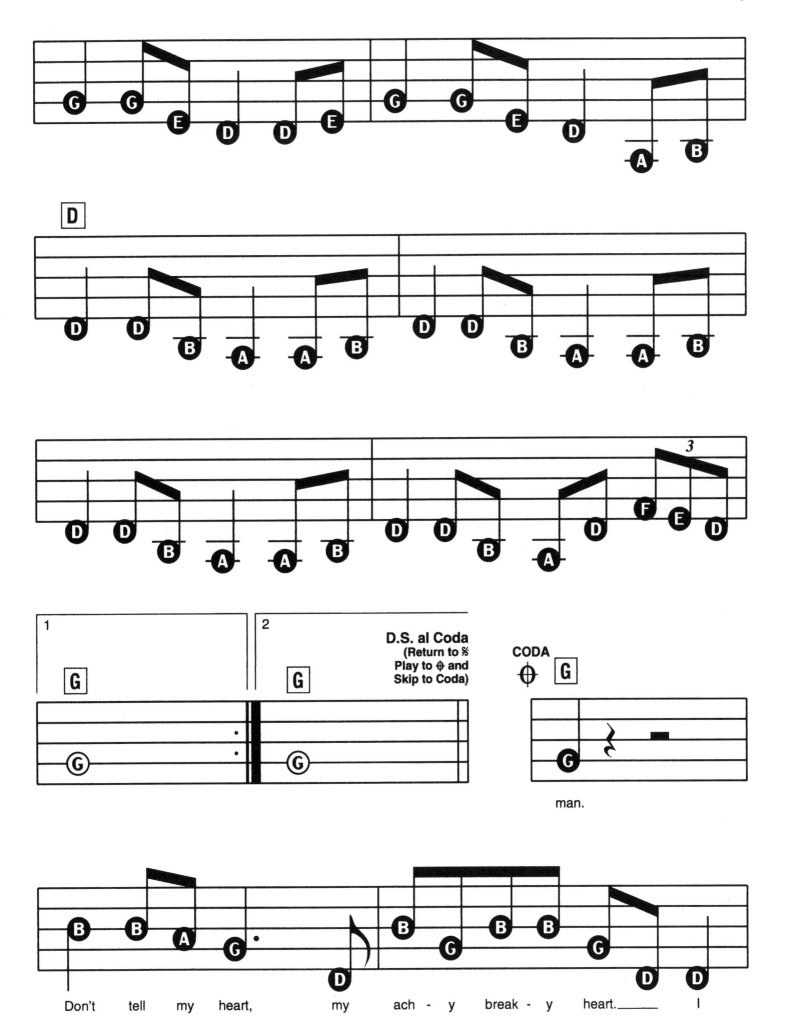

Don't tell my heart, my ach - y break - y heart._____ I

man.

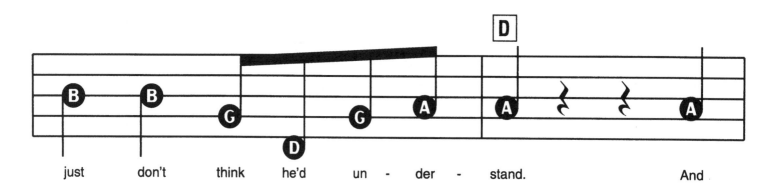

just don't think he'd un - der - stand. And

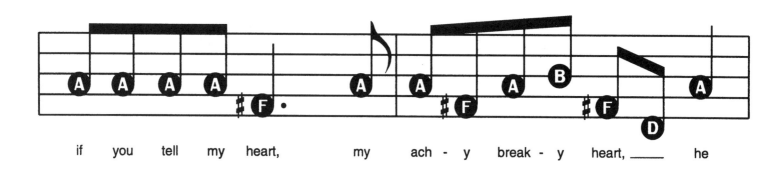

if you tell my heart, my ach - y break - y heart, _____ he

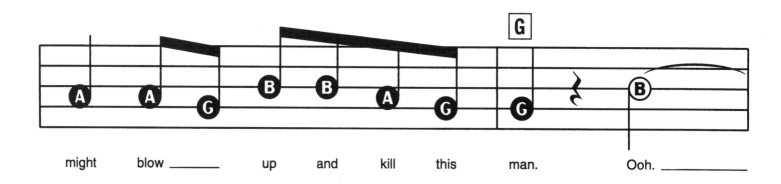

might blow _____ up and kill this man. Ooh. _____

Bo Diddley

Registration 4
Rhythm: Fox Trot or Swing

Words and Music by
Ellas McDaniel

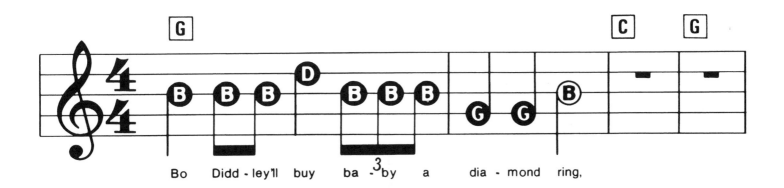

Bo   Didd - ley'll   buy   ba - by   a   dia - mond   ring,

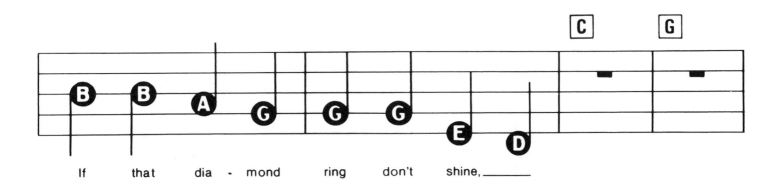

If   that   dia - mond   ring   don't   shine, _____

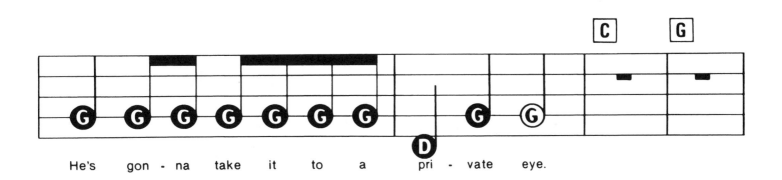

He's   gon - na   take   it   to   a   pri - vate   eye.

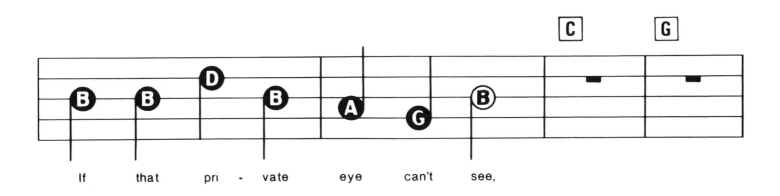

If   that   pri - vate   eye   can't   see,

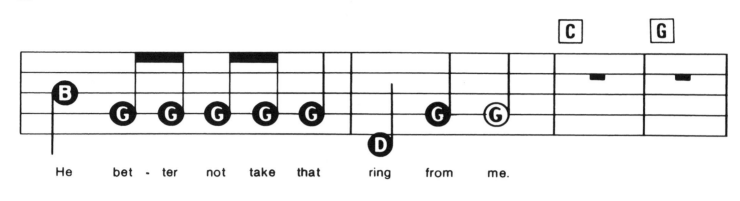

He bet - ter not take that ring from me.

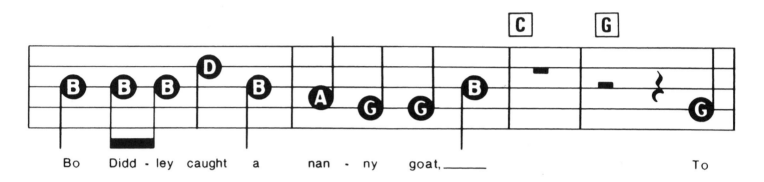

Bo Didd - ley caught a nan - ny goat,_____ To

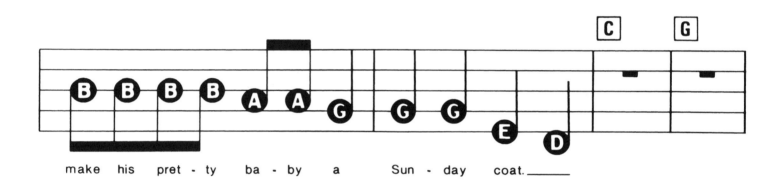

make his pret - ty ba - by a Sun - day coat._____

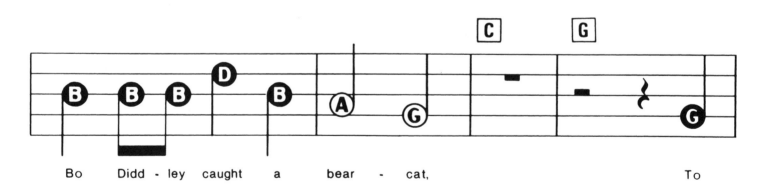

Bo Didd - ley caught a bear - cat, To

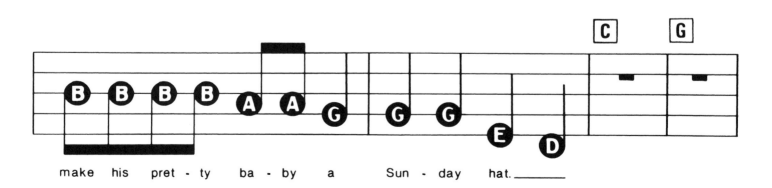

make his pret - ty ba - by a Sun - day hat._____

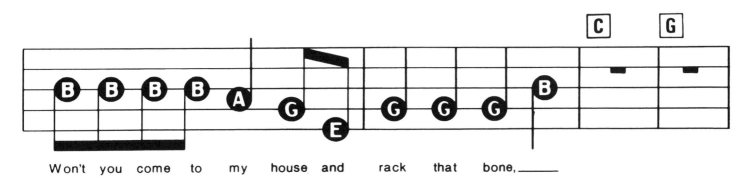

Won't you come to my house and rack that bone,_____

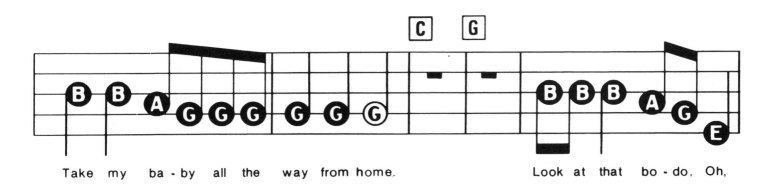

Take my ba - by all the way from home.　Look at that bo - do, Oh,

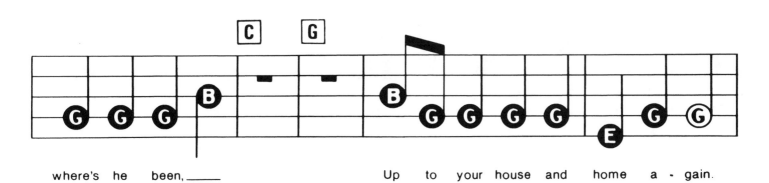

where's he been,_____　Up to your house and home a - gain.

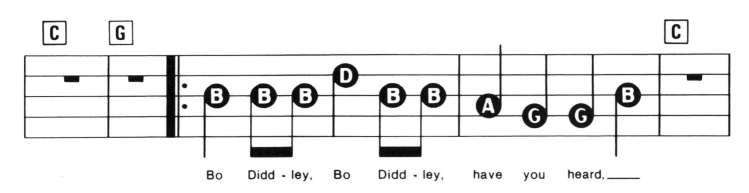

Bo Didd - ley, Bo Didd - ley, have you heard,_____

Repeat and Fade

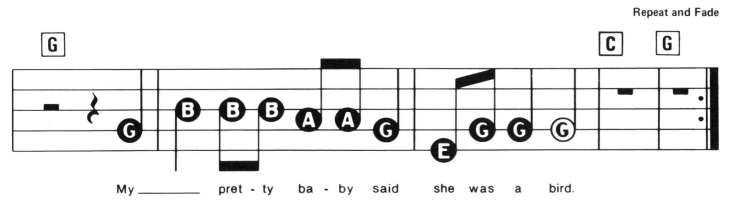

My _____ pret - ty ba - by said she was a bird.

Day-O
(The Banana Boat Song)

Registration 5
Rhythm: Latin

Words and Music by Irving Burgie
and William Attaway

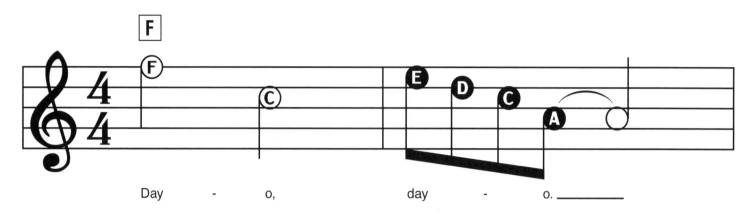

Day - o, day - o. _____

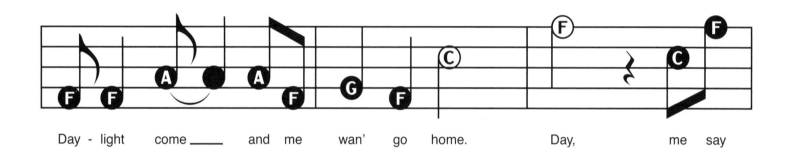

Day - light come ____ and me wan' go home. Day, me say

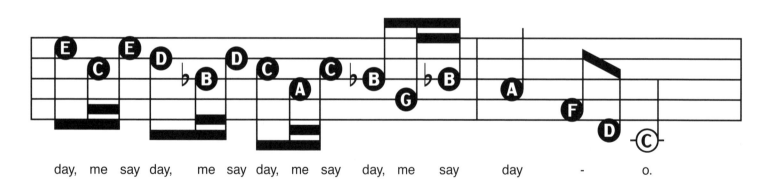

day, me say day, me say day, me say day, me say day - o.

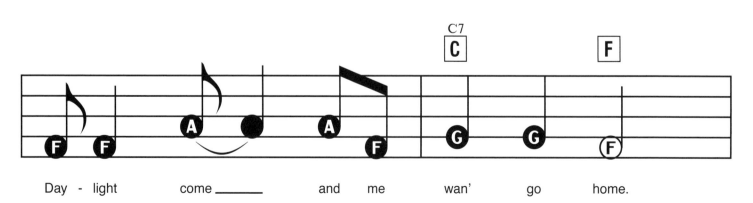

Day - light come _____ and me wan' go home.

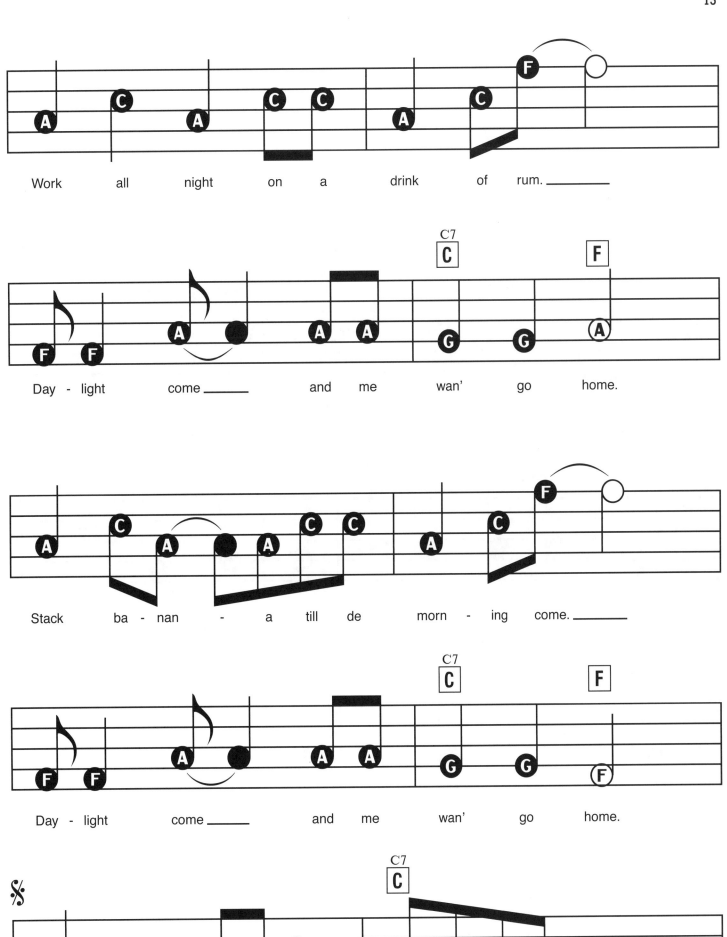

Work all night on a drink of rum. _____

Day - light come _____ and me wan' go home.

Stack ba - nan - a till de morn - ing come. _____

Day - light come _____ and me wan' go home.

Come, mis - ter tal - ly man, tal - ly me ba - nan - a.

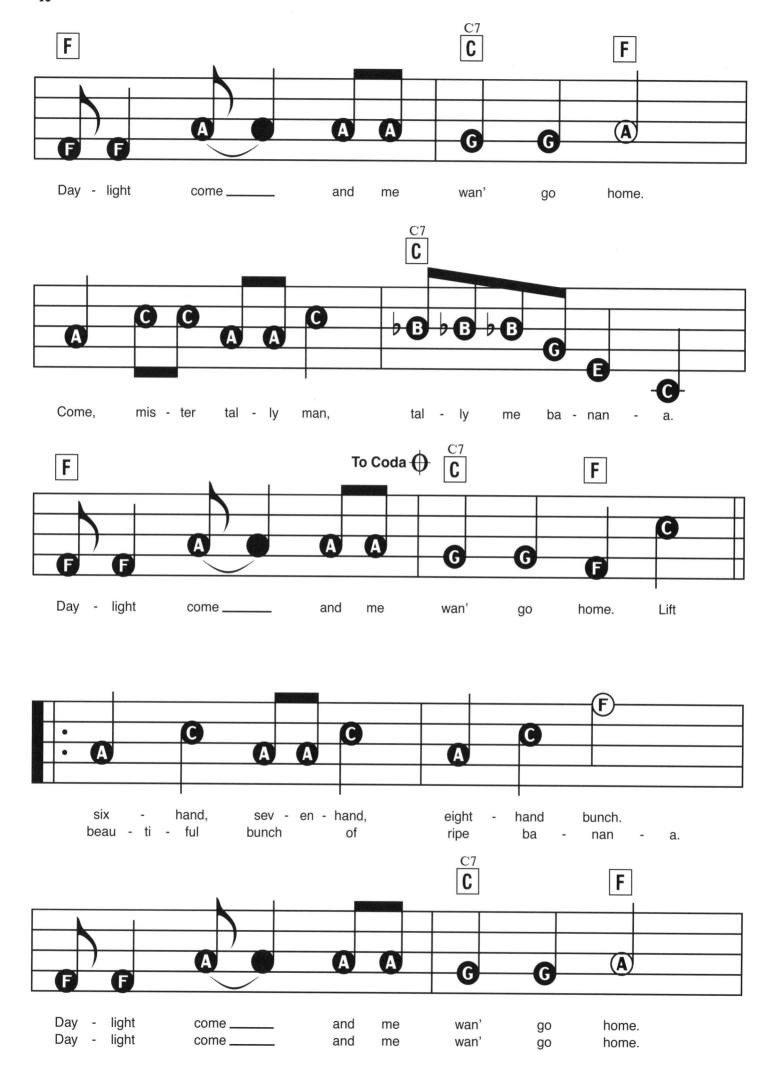

Six - hand, sev - en - hand, eight - hand bunch.
Hide the dead - ly black ta - ran - t'la.

Day - light come _____ and me wan' go home. }
Day - light come _____ and me wan' go home. }

Day, me say day - o. _____

Day - light come _____ and me wan' go home.

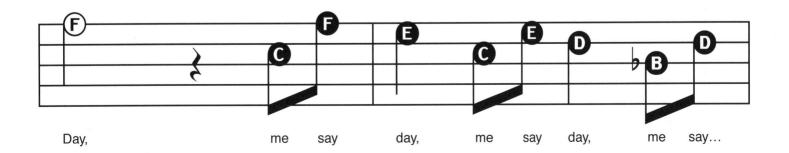

Day, me say day, me say day, me say…

18

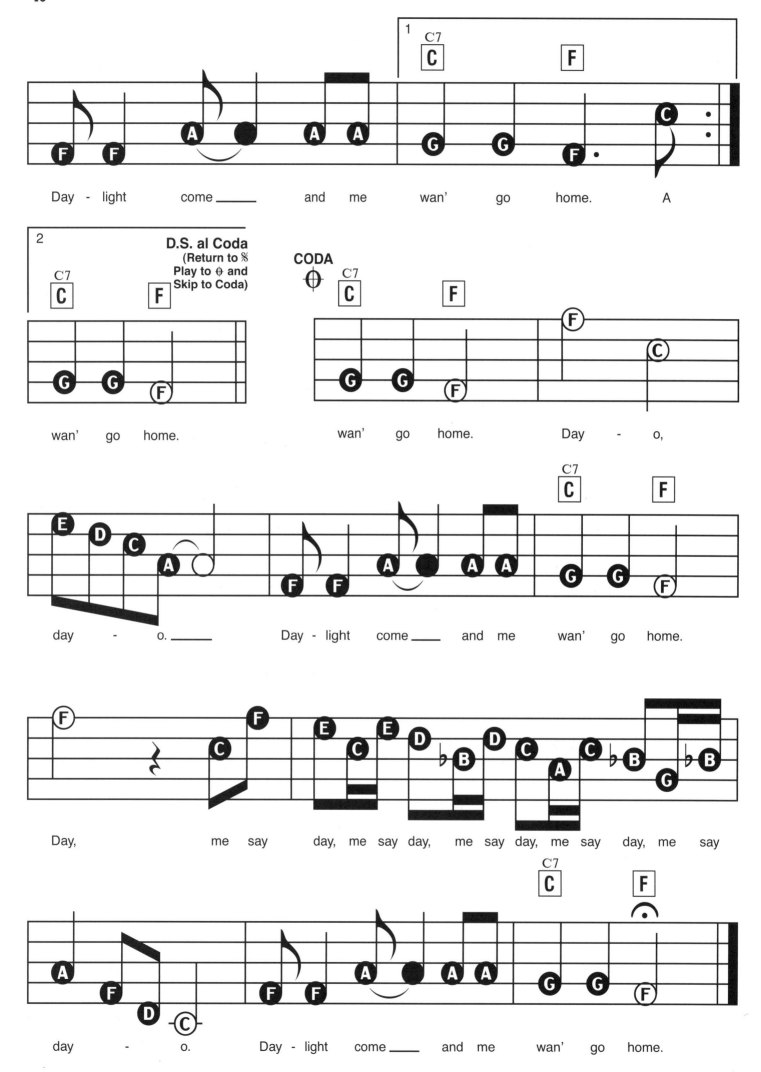

Feelin' Alright

Registration 4
Rhythm: Rock

Words and Music by
Dave Mason

It seems I've got to have a change of scene, _____
Well, boy, you sure took me for one big ride, _____

'cause ev - 'ry night I have the strang - est dream. _____
and e - ven now I sit and won - der why. _____

Then Pris - oned by the way it could have been.
when I think of you I start to cry.

Left here on my own, or so it seems. _____
I just can't waste my time, I must keep dry. _____

I've got to leave here 'fore I start to scream, _____
Got - ta stop be - liev - in' in all your lies, _____

20

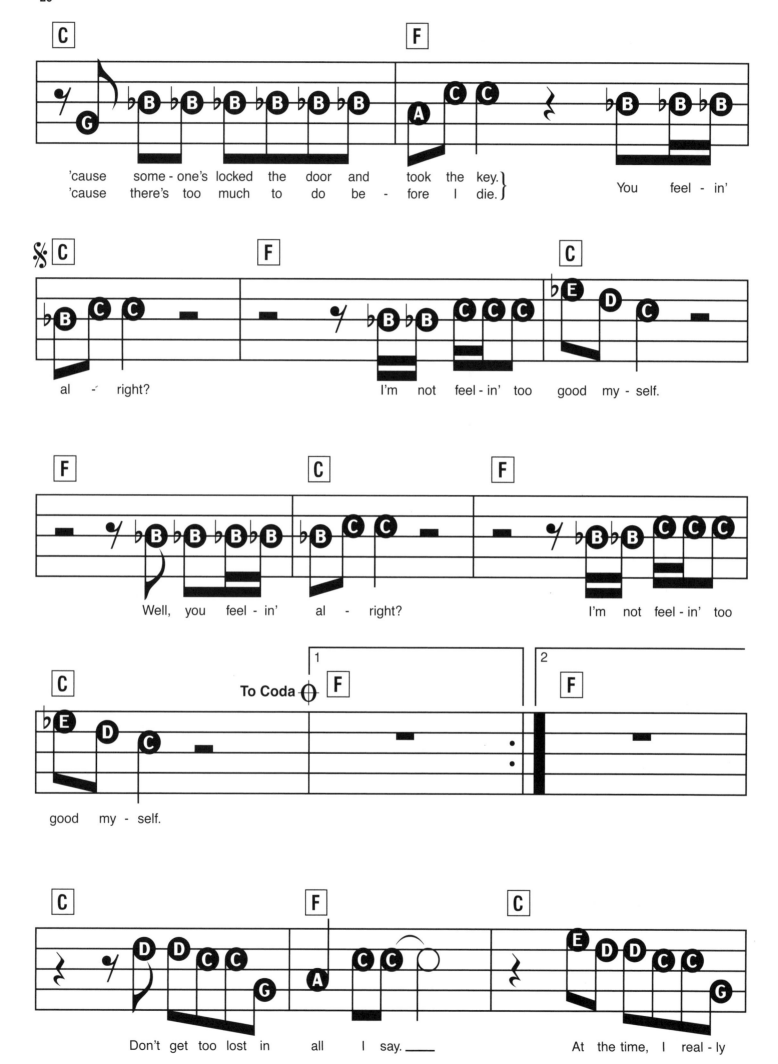

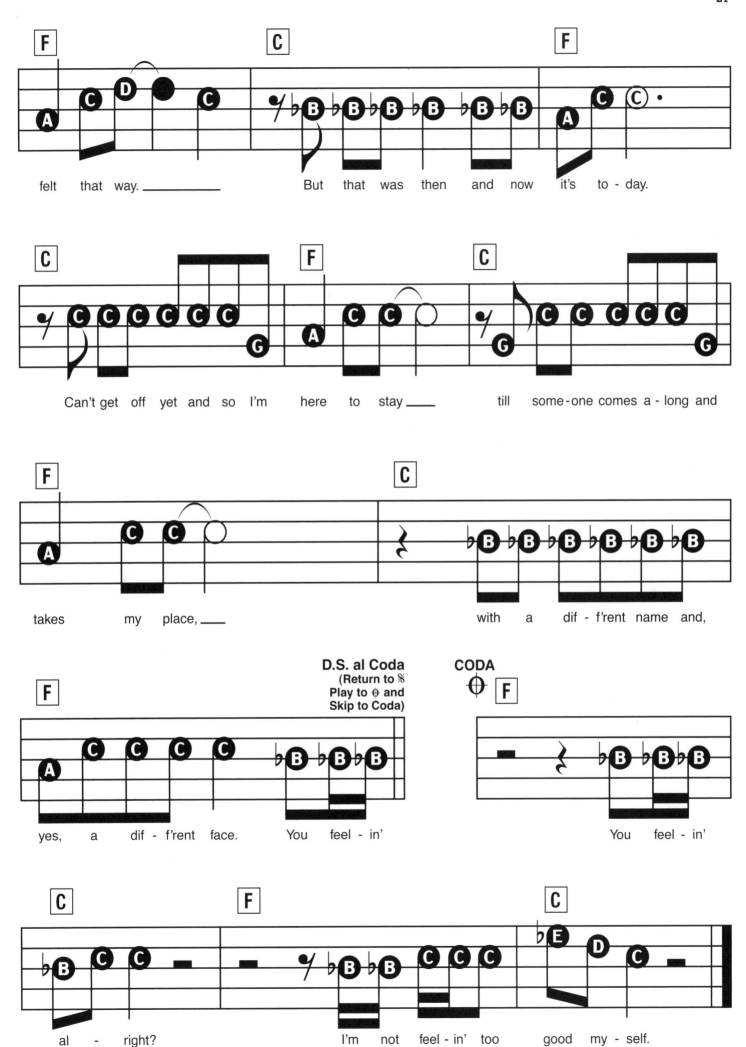

Deep in the Heart of Texas

Registration 4
Rhythm: Country or Fox Trot

Words by June Hershey
Music by Don Swander

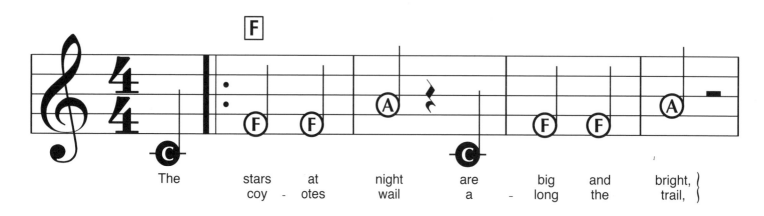

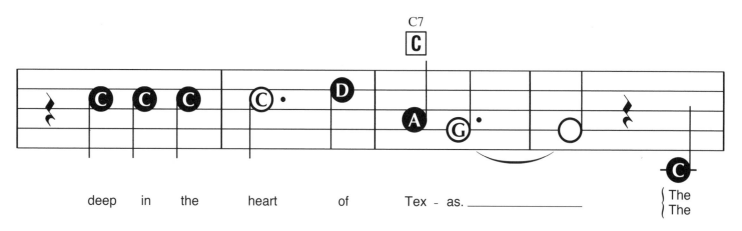

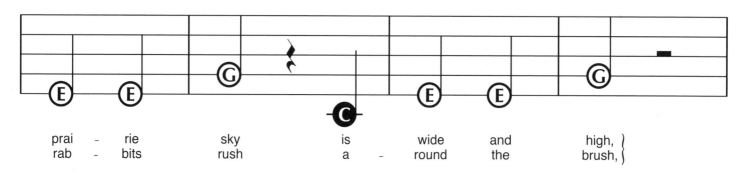

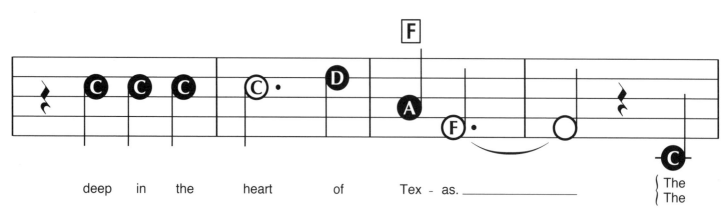

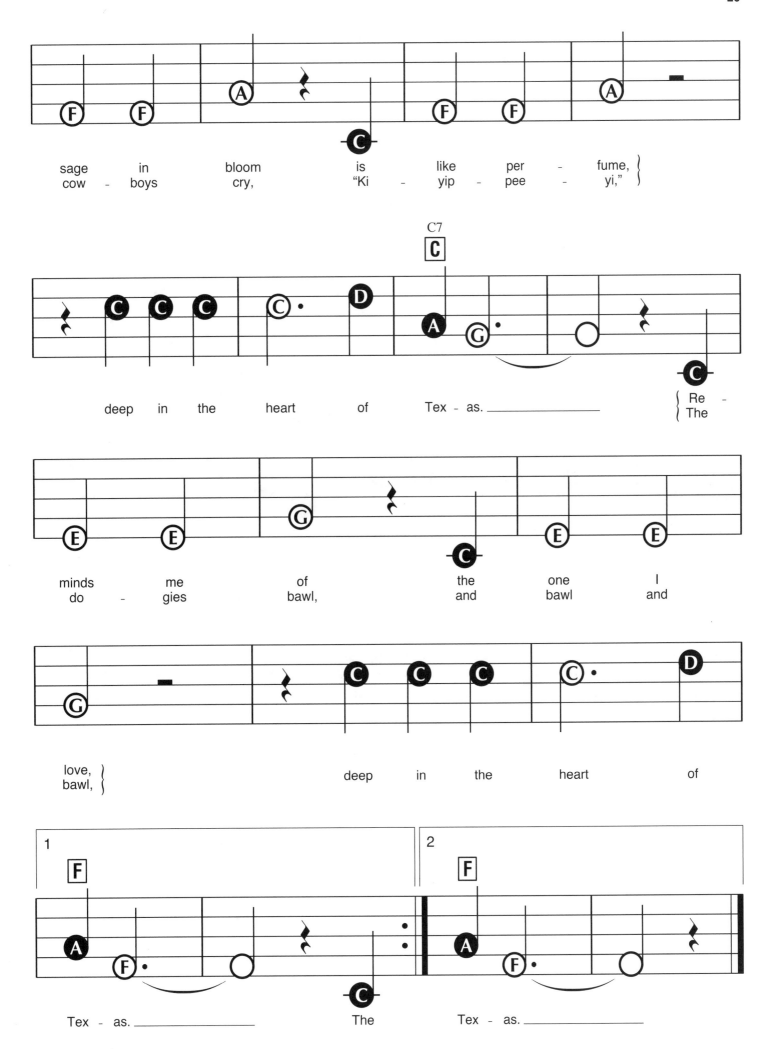

Dream Baby
(How Long Must I Dream)

Registration 7
Rhythm: Ballad or Fox Trot

Words and Music by
Cindy Walker

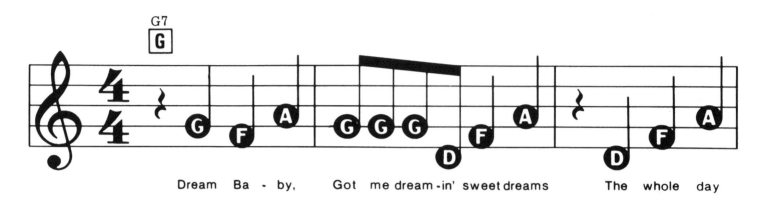

Dream Ba - by, Got me dream-in' sweet dreams The whole day

through. Dream Ba - by, Got me dream - in' sweet dreams Night time,

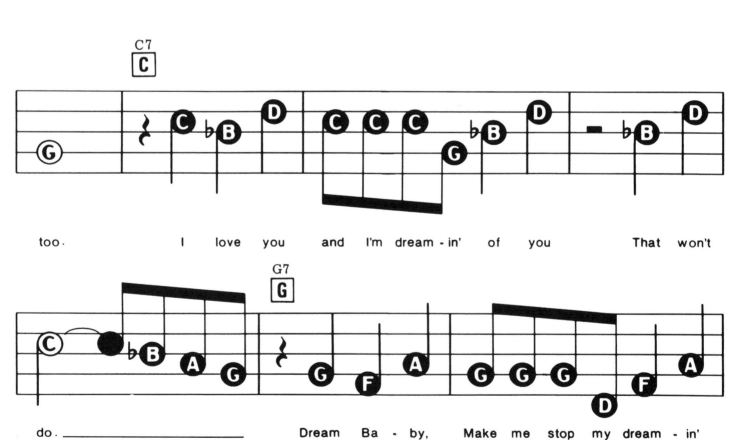

too. I love you and I'm dream-in' of you That won't

do. _____ Dream Ba - by, Make me stop my dream - in'

Eleanor Rigby

Registration 9
Rhythm: Rock

Words and Music by John Lennon
and Paul McCartney

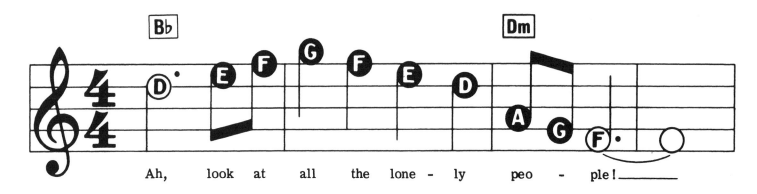

Ah, look at all the lone - ly peo - ple! _____

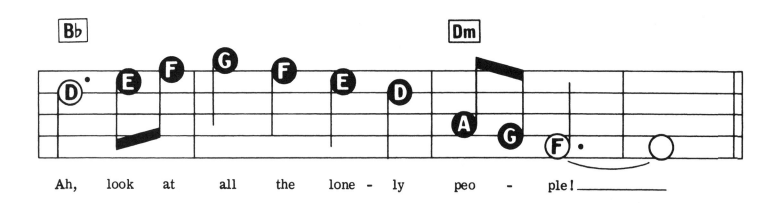

Ah, look at all the lone - ly peo - ple! _____

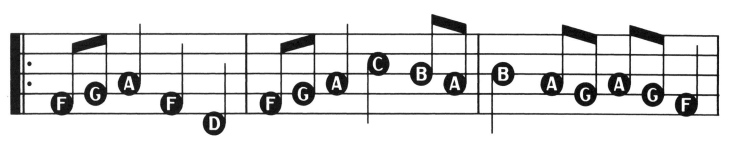

E - lea - nor Rig - by, picks up the rice in the church where a wed - ding has
E - lea - nor Rig - by, died in the church and was bur - ied a - long with her

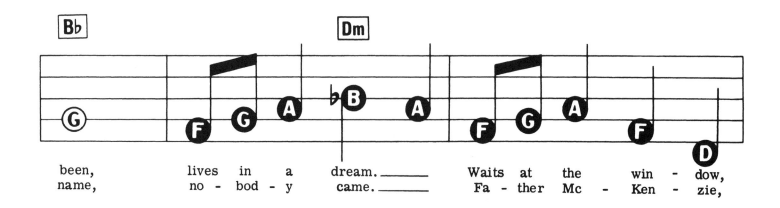

been, lives in a dream. _____ Waits at the win - dow,
name, no - bod - y came. _____ Fa - ther Mc - Ken - zie,

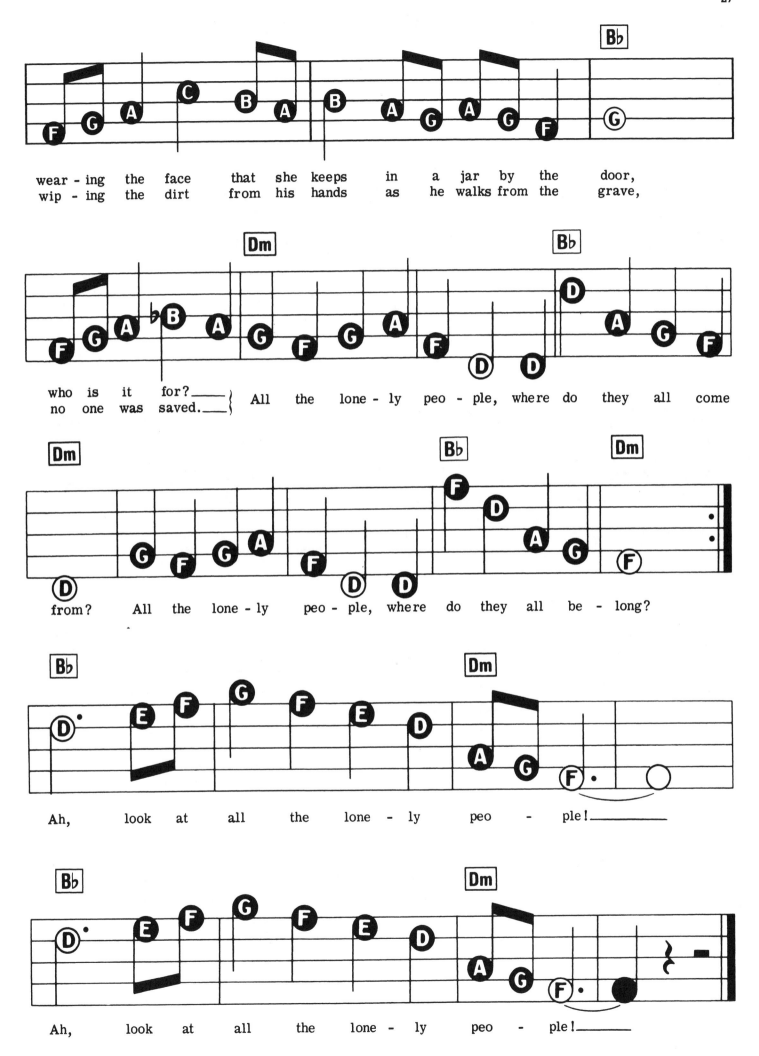

Get Down Tonight

Registration 4
Rhythm: Rock

Words and Music by Harry Wayne Casey
and Richard Finch

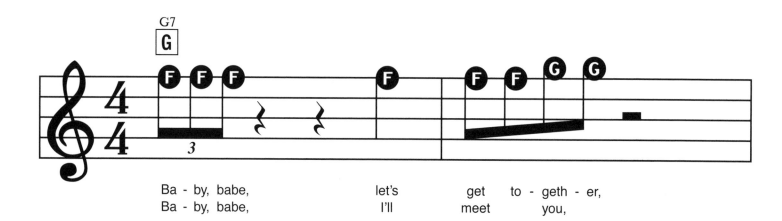

Ba - by, babe,   let's   get   to - geth - er,
Ba - by, babe,   I'll   get   meet   you,

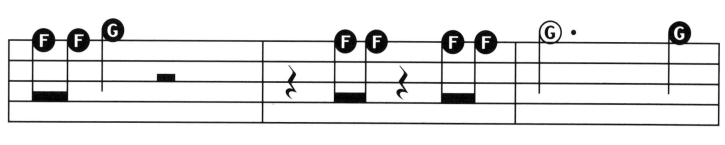

hon - ey, hon - ey,   me and   you,   and   do the things,   oh,
same place,   same time   where   we   can,   oh,

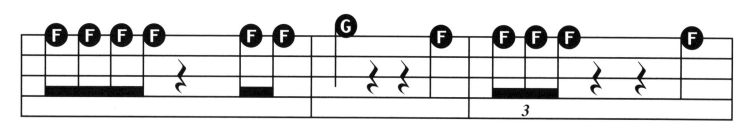

do the things   that we   like to   do.
get to - geth - er and   ease up   our   mind.   Oh,

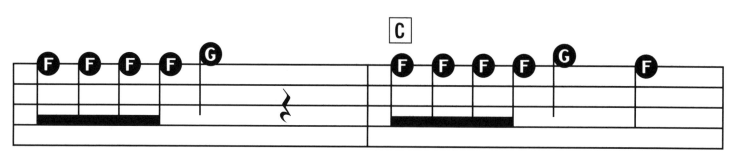

do a lit - tle dance,   make a lit - tle love,   get

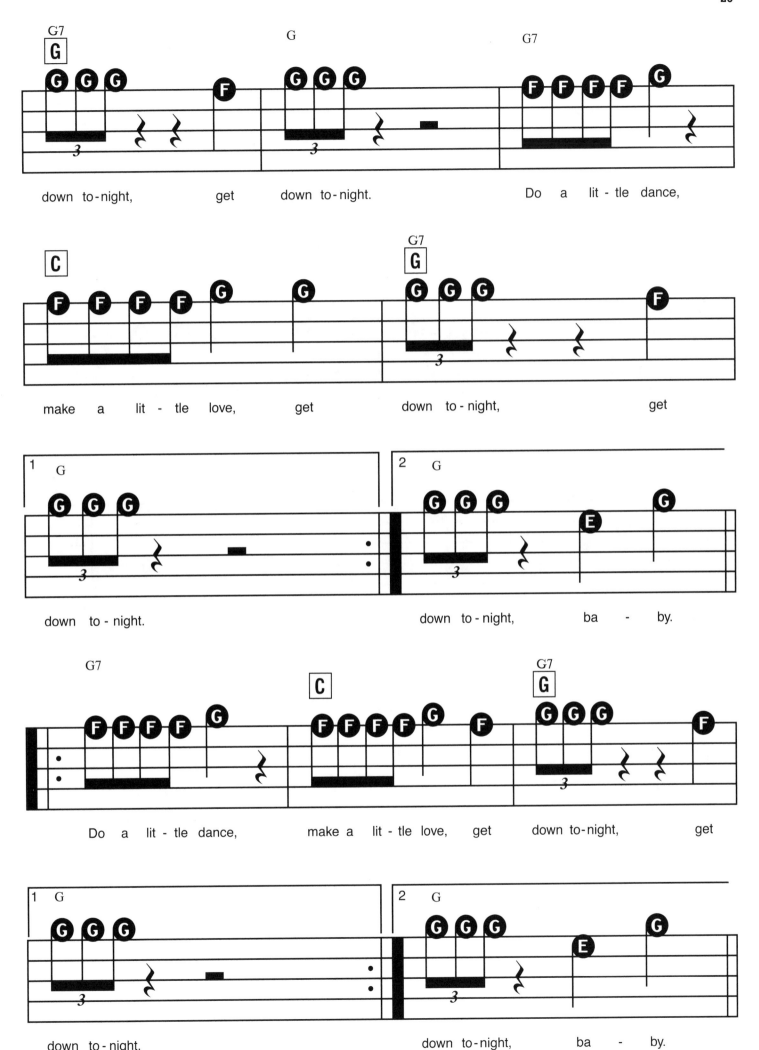

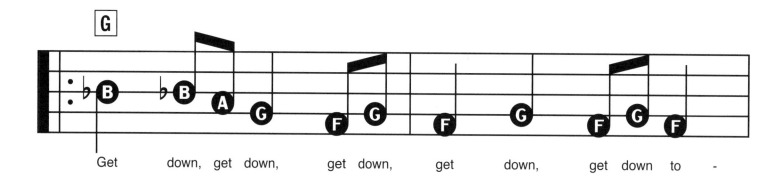

Get down, get down, get down, get down, get down to -

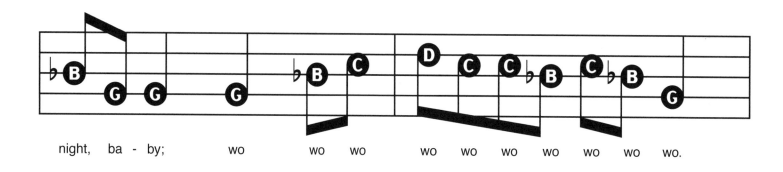

night, ba - by; wo wo wo wo wo wo wo wo wo wo.

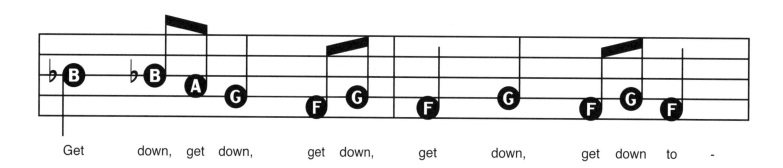

Get down, get down, get down, get down, get down to -

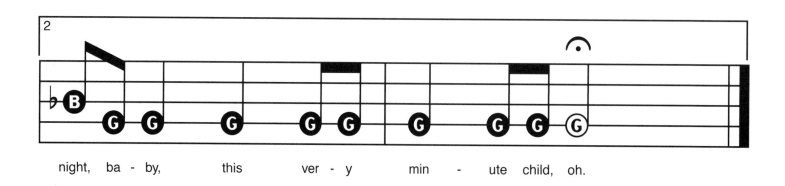

night, ba - by; na na na na na na na na na na.

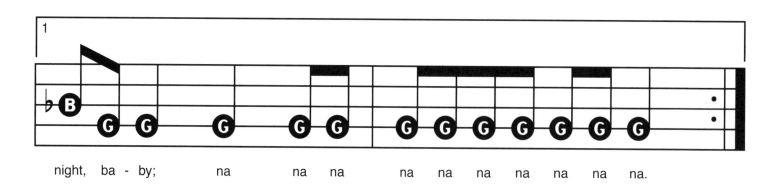

night, ba - by, this ver - y min - ute child, oh.

Hey Liley, Liley Lo
(Married Man Gonna Keep Your Secret)

Registration 4
Rhythm: Fox Trot

Words and Music by Elizabeth Austin
and Alan Lomax
Additional Words and Music by Alan Lomax

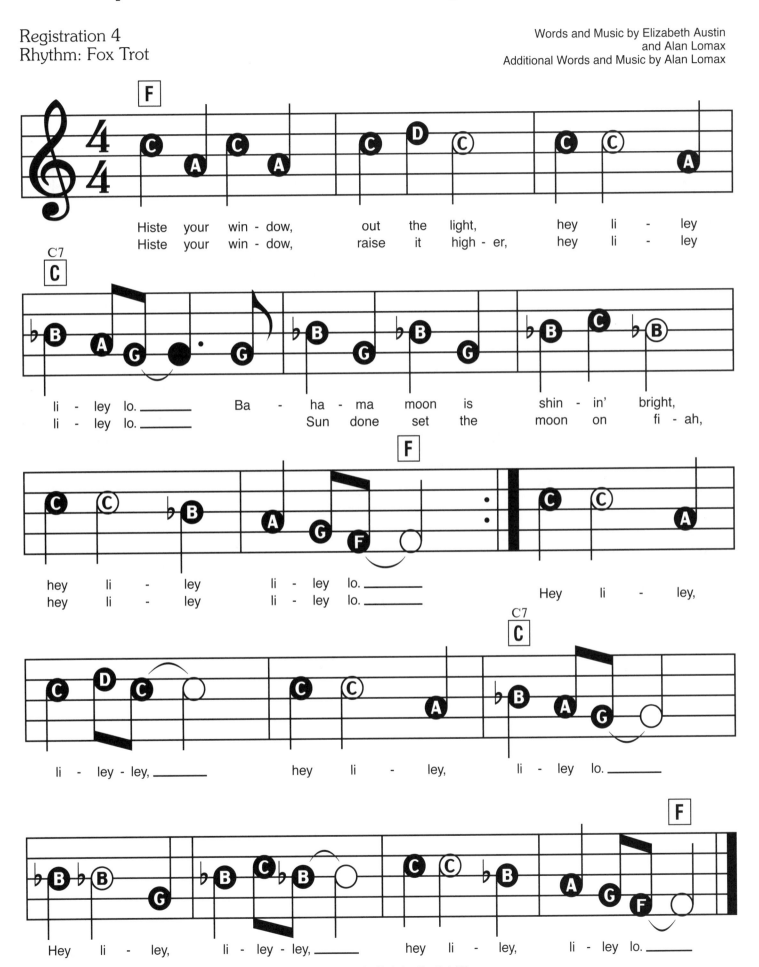

The Hokey Pokey

Registration 5
Rhythm: Fox Trot or Swing

Words and Music by Charles P. Macak,
Tafft Baker and Larry LaPrise

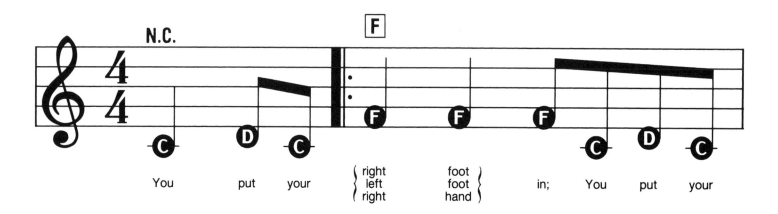

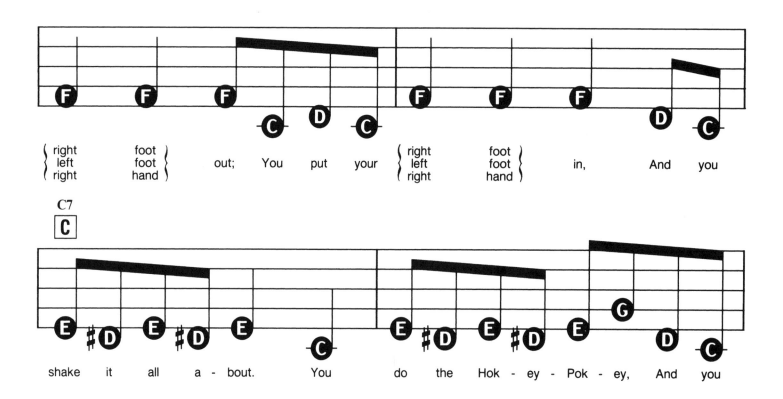

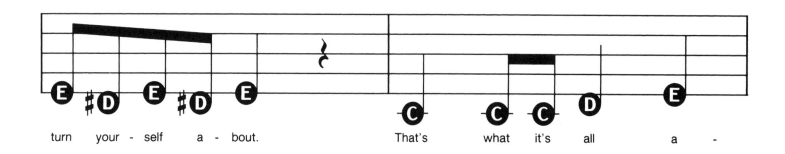

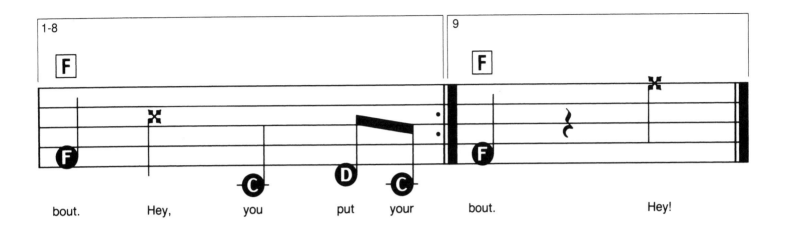

bout.   Hey,   you   put   your   bout.   Hey!

Additional Lyrics

4. Hey, you put your left hand in;
You put your left hand out;
You put your left hand in,
And you shake it all about.
You do the Hokey-Pokey,
And you turn yourself about.
That's what it's all about.

5. Hey, you put your right shoulder in;
You put your right shoulder out;
Etc.

6. Hey, you put your left shoulder in;
You put your left shoulder out;
Etc.

7. Hey, you put your right hip in;
You put your right hip out;
Etc.

8. Hey, you put your left hip in;
You put your left hip out;
Etc.

9. Hey, you put your whole self in;
You put your whole self out;
Etc.

Honky Tonkin'

Registration 8
Rhythm: Country, Fox Trot or Swing

Words and Music by
Hank Williams

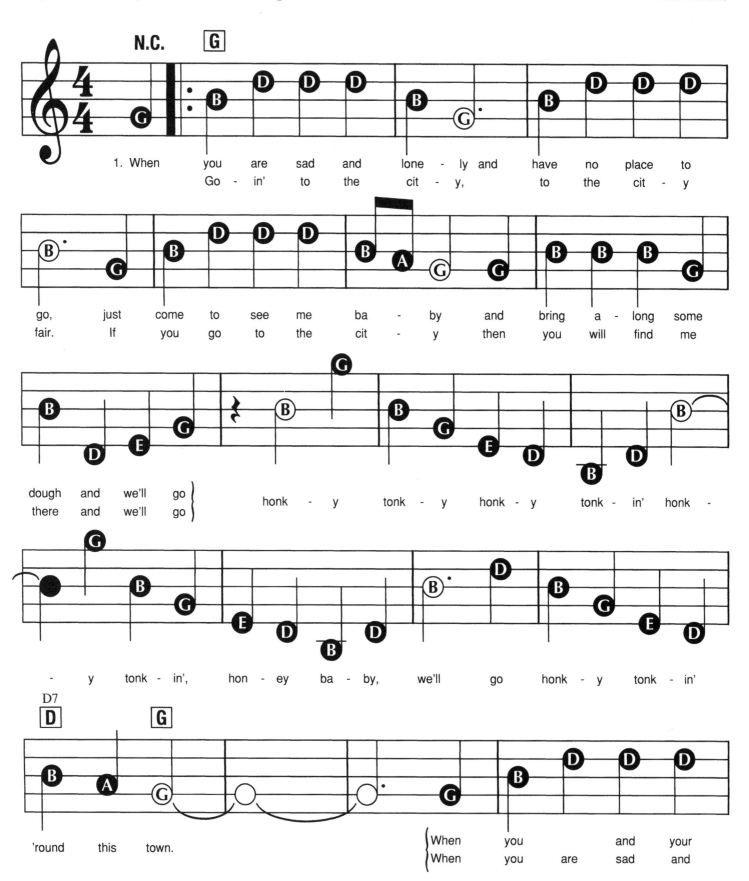

A Horse with No Name

Registration 10
Rhythm: Rock or Slow Rock

Words and Music by
Dewey Bunnell

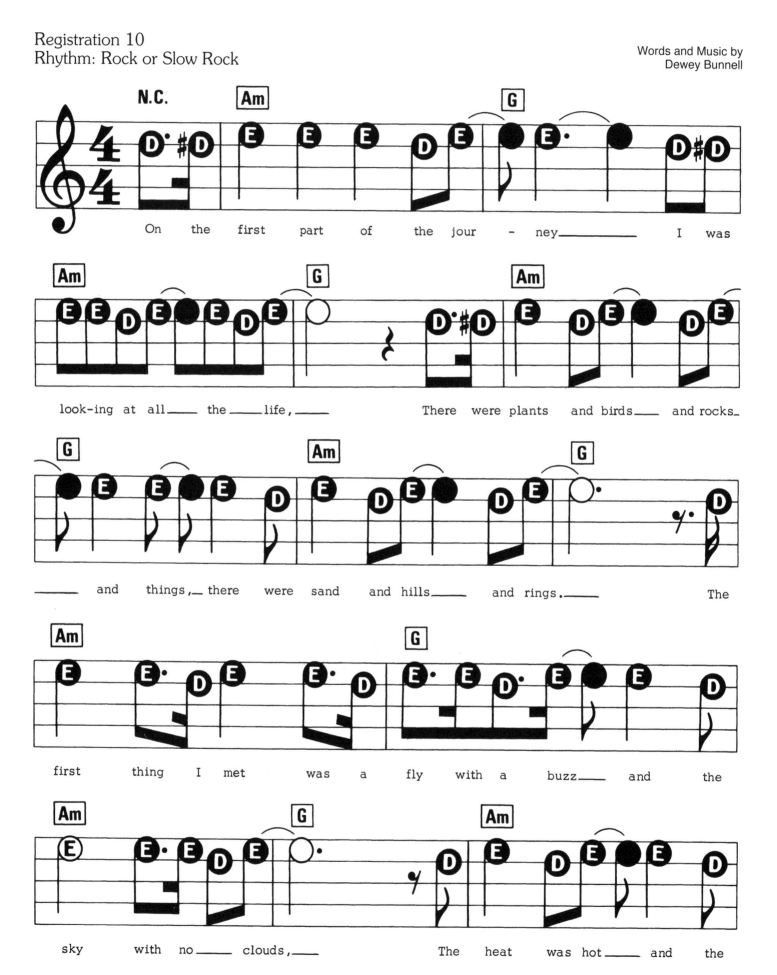

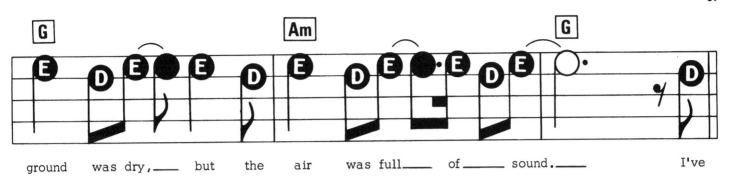

ground was dry,___ but the air was full___ of ___ sound.___ I've

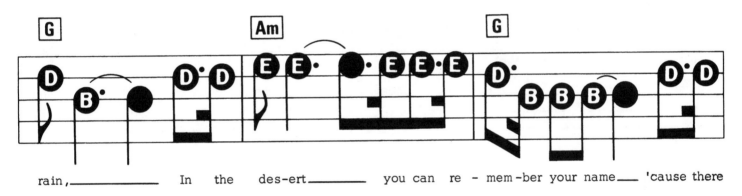

been thru the des-ert on a horse with no name,___ it felt good to be out___ of the

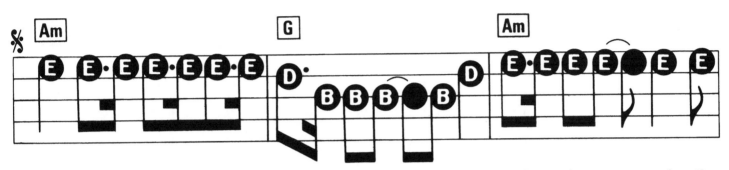

rain,_____ In the des-ert_____ you can re - mem-ber your name___ 'cause there

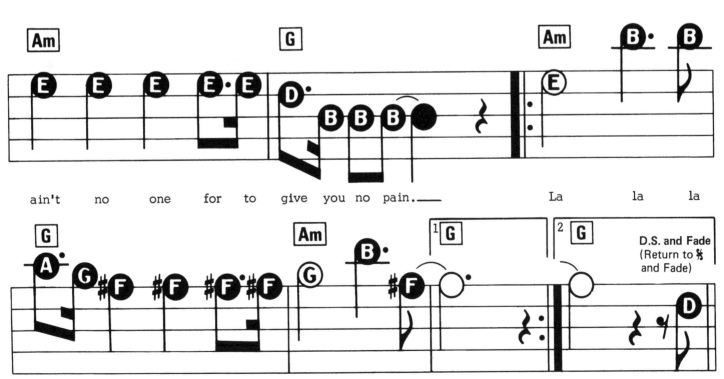

ain't no one for to give you no pain.___ La la la

la la la la la la la la.___ ___ I've

I Love You a Thousand Ways

Registration 4
Rhythm: Country

Words and Music by Lefty Frizzell
and James A. Beck

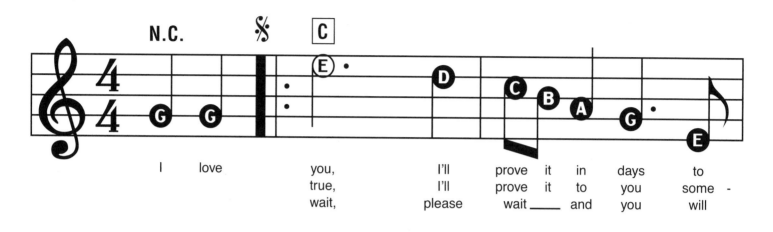

I love you, I'll prove it in days to
true, I'll prove it to you some -
wait, please wait ____ and you will

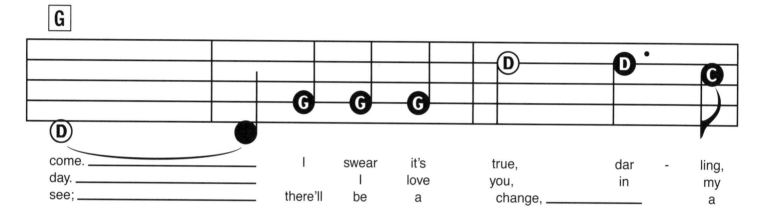

come. ____ I swear it's true, dar - ling,
day. ____ I love you, in my
see; ____ there'll be a change, ____ a

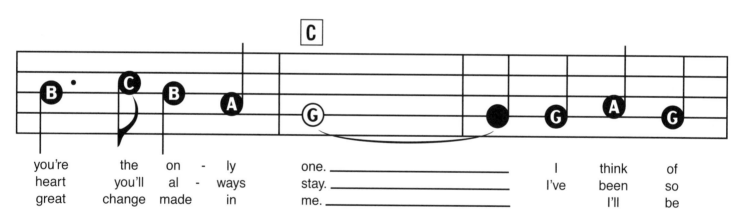

you're the on - ly one. ____ I think of
heart you'll al - ways stay. ____ I've been so
great change made in me. ____ I'll be

To Coda ⊕

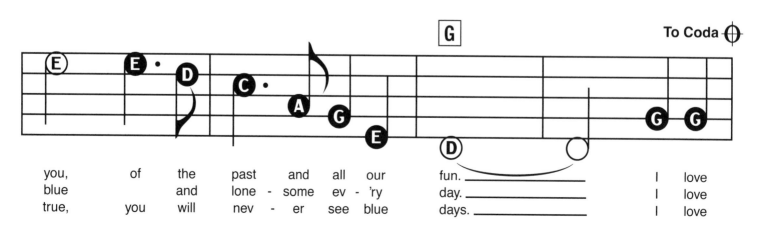

you, of the past and all our fun. ____ I love
blue and lone - some ev - 'ry day. ____ I love
true, you will nev - er see blue days. ____ I love

I'd Rather Go Blind

Registration 1
Rhythm: Waltz

Words and Music by Ellington Jordan
and Billy Foster

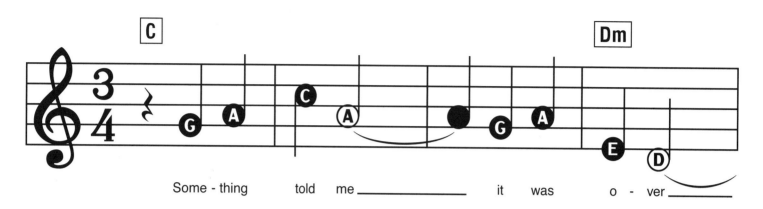

Some - thing told me _____ it was o - ver _____

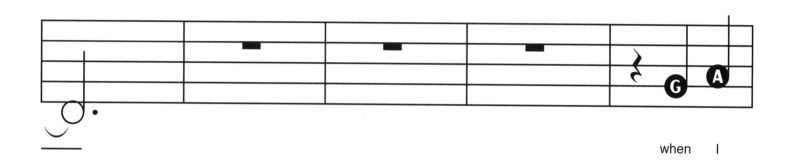

_____ when I

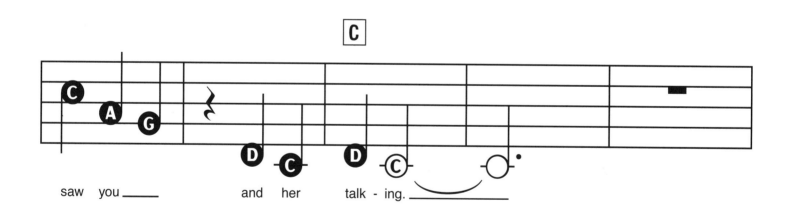

saw you _____ and her talk - ing. _____

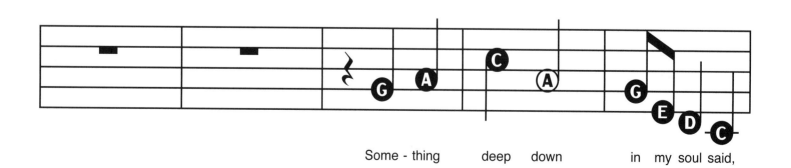

Some - thing deep down in my soul said,

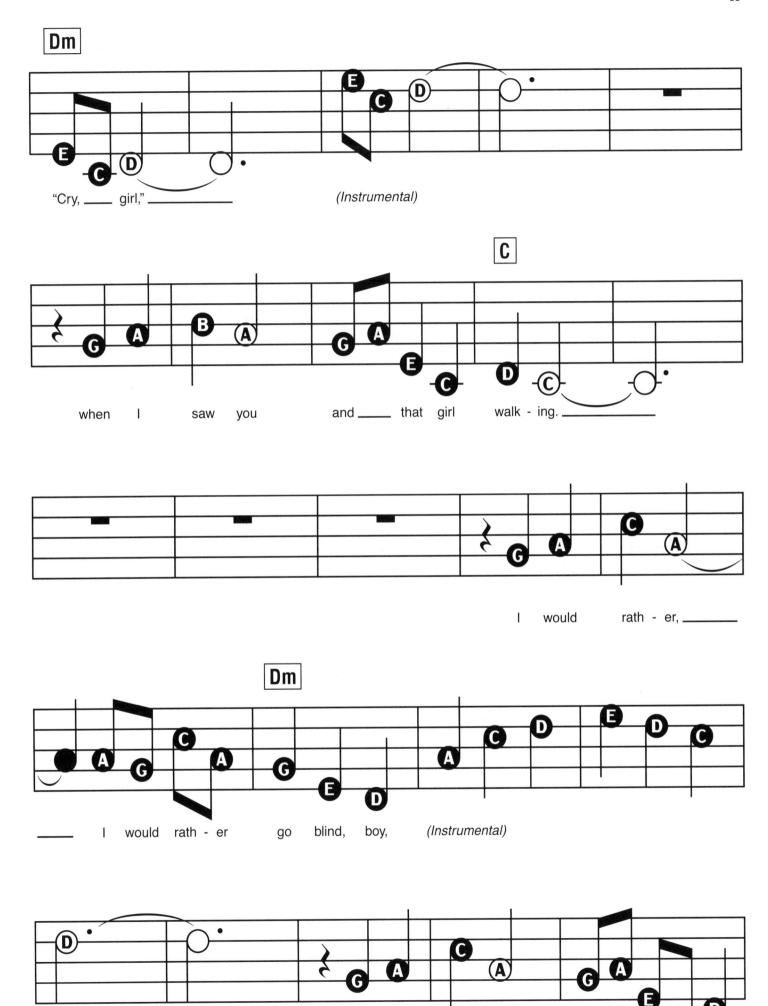

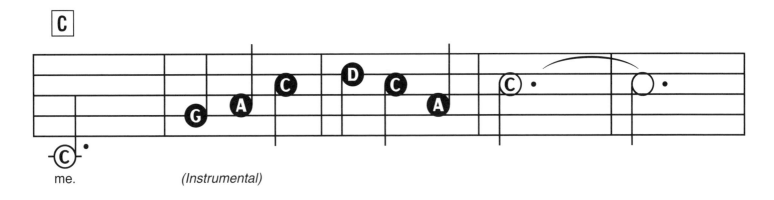

me. (Instrumental)

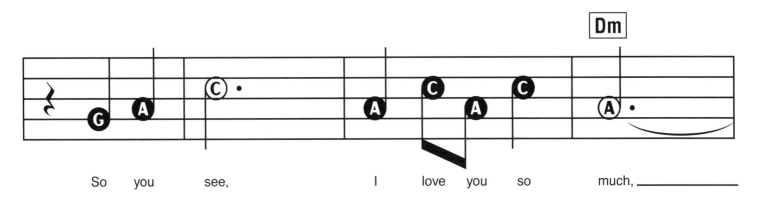

So you see, I love you so much,_____

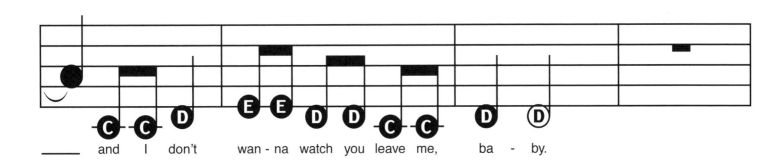

_____ and I don't wan-na watch you leave me, ba - by.

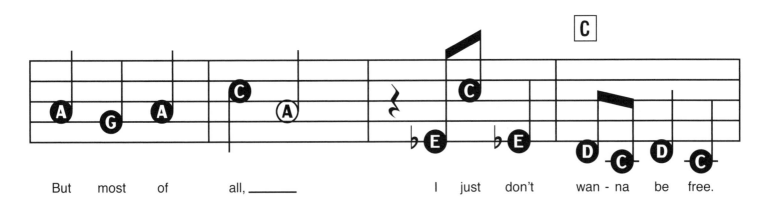

But most of all,_____ I just don't wan-na be free.

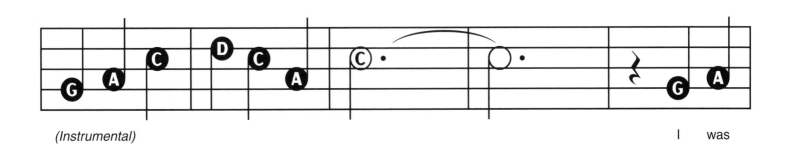

(Instrumental) I was

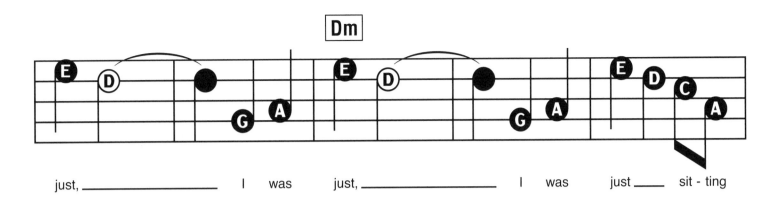

just, _____ I was just, _____ I was just ____ sit - ting

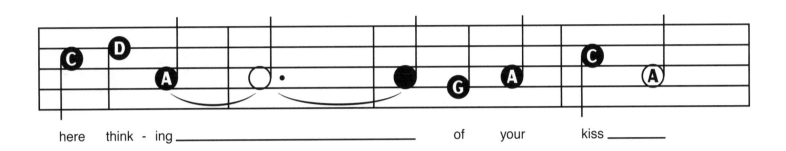

here think - ing _____ of your kiss _____

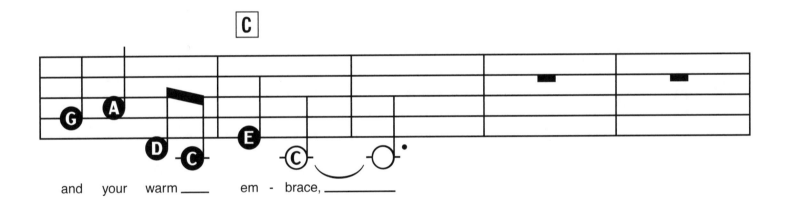

and your warm ___ em - brace, _____

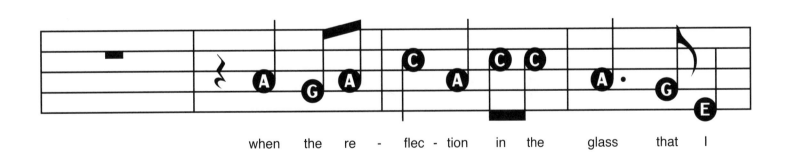

when the re - flec - tion in the glass that I

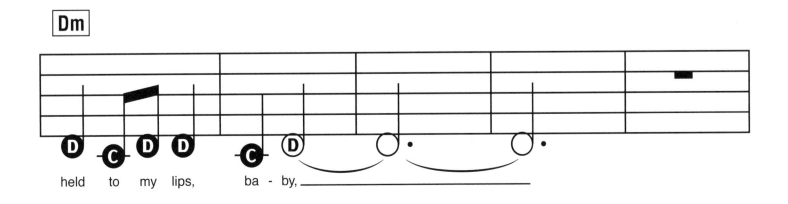

held to my lips, ba - by, _____

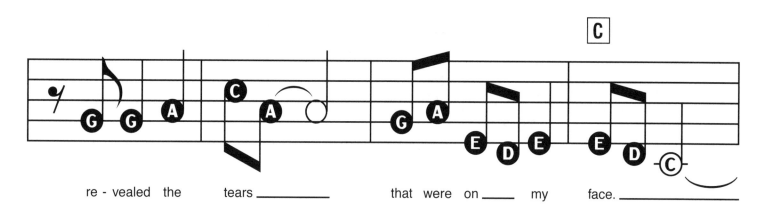

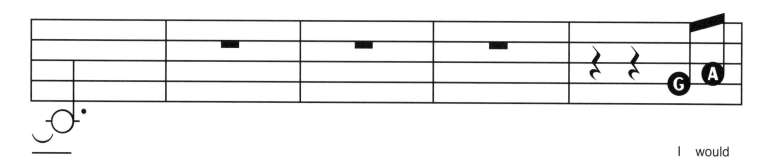

re - vealed the tears _____ that were on _____ my face. _____

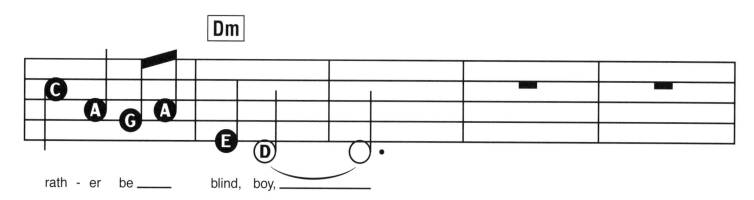

I would

rath - er be _____ blind, boy, _____

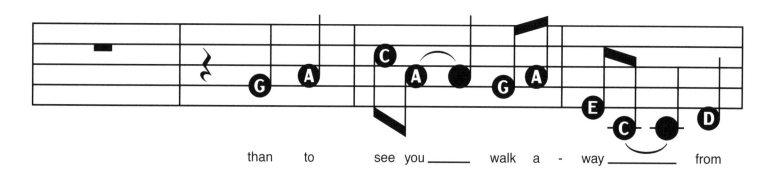

than to see you _____ walk a - way _____ from

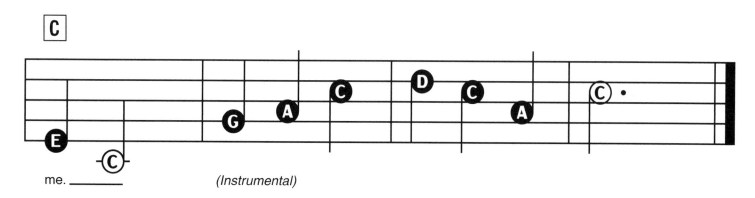

me. _____ *(Instrumental)*

It's Your Thing

Registration 9
Rhythm: Funk or Rock

Words and Music by Rudolph Isley,
Ronald Isley and O'Kelly Isley

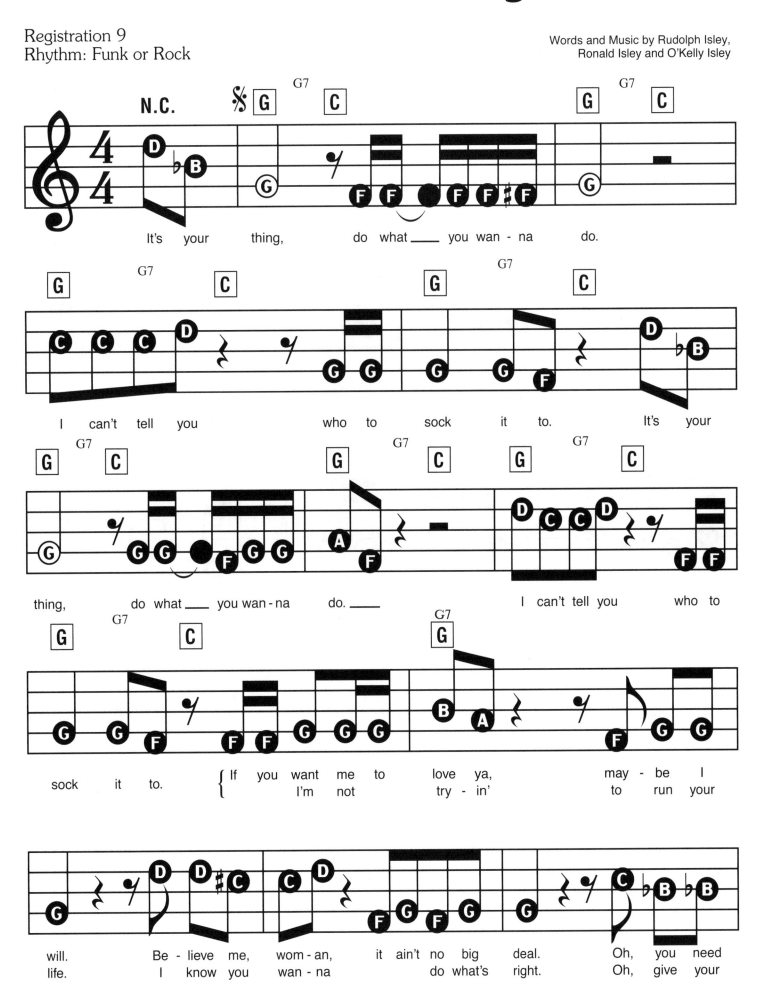

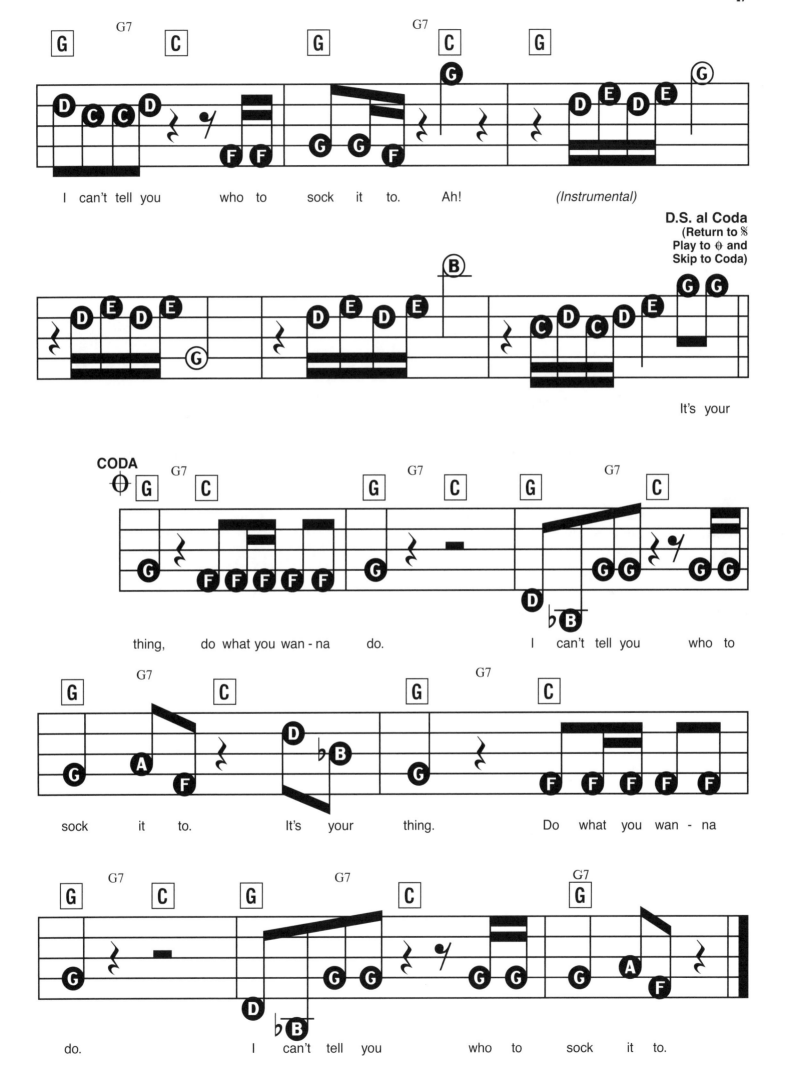

Jambalaya
(On the Bayou)

Registration 4
Rhythm: Fox Trot

Words and Music by
Hank Williams

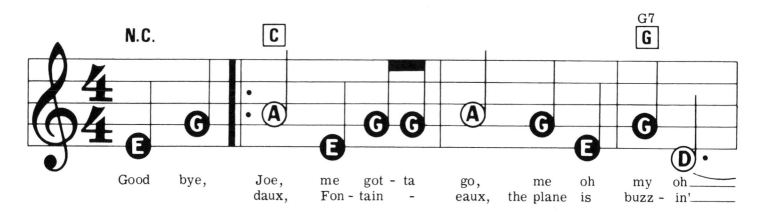

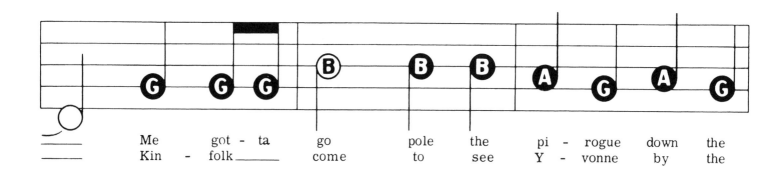

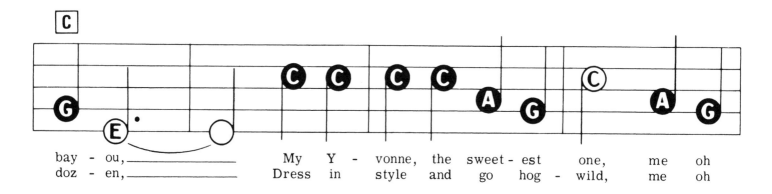

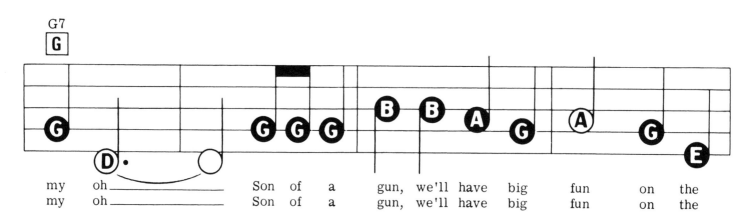

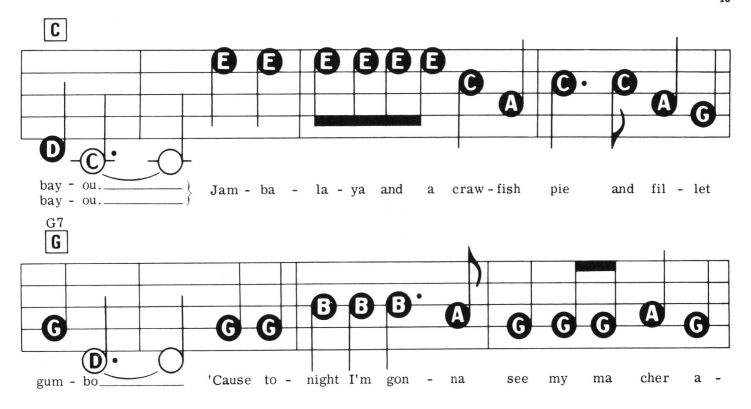

bay - ou. _____
bay - ou. _____ } Jam - ba - la - ya and a craw-fish pie and fil - let

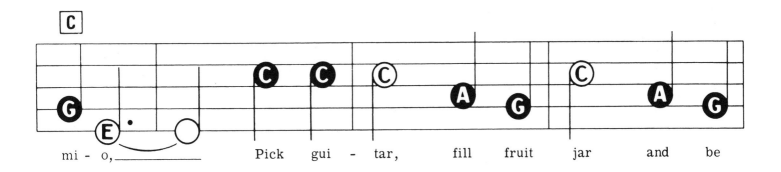

gum - bo _____ 'Cause to - night I'm gon - na see my ma cher a -

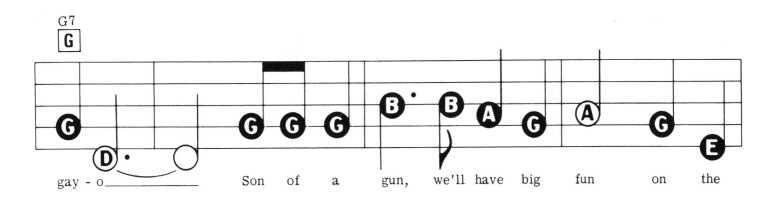

mi - o, _____ Pick gui - tar, fill fruit jar and be

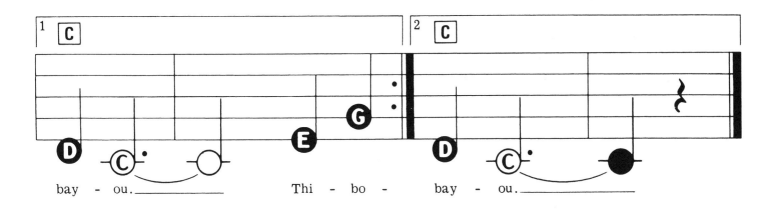

gay - o _____ Son of a gun, we'll have big fun on the

bay - ou. _____ Thi - bo - bay - ou. _____

Okie from Muskogee

Registration 4
Rhythm: Country or Shuffle

Words and Music by Merle Haggard
and Roy Edward Burris

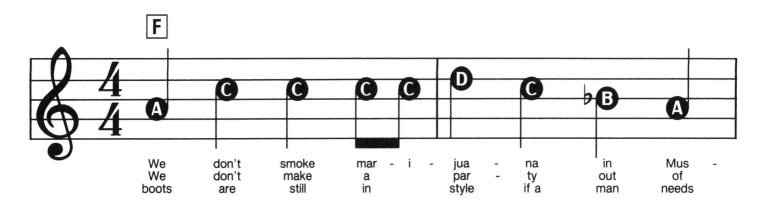

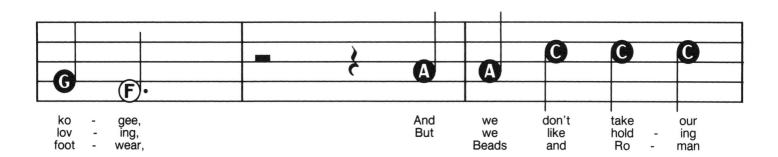

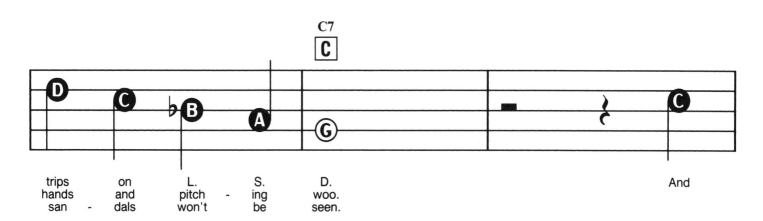

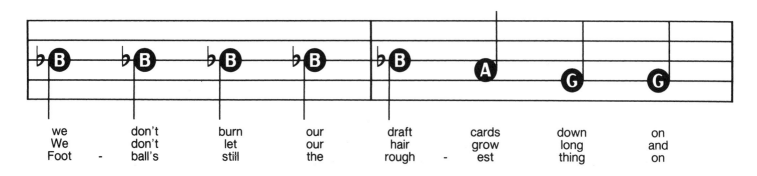

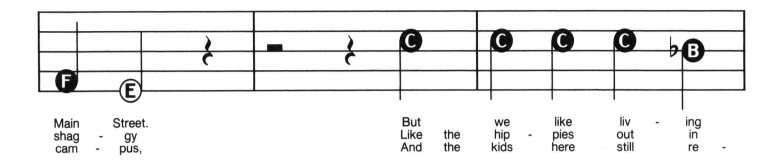

Main Street.
shag - gy
cam - pus,

But   we   like   liv - ing
Like the   hip - pies   out   in
And the   kids   here   still   re -

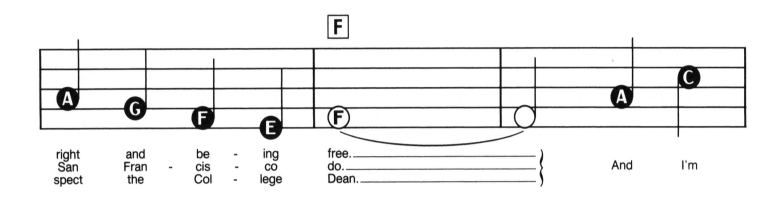

right   and   be - ing   free._____   } And   I'm
San   Fran - cis - co   do._____
spect the   Col - lege   Dean._____

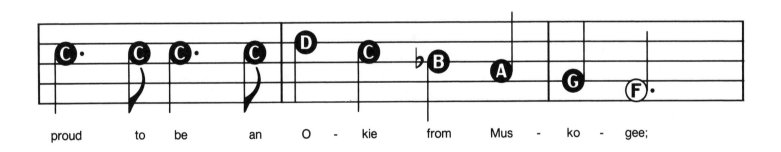

proud   to   be   an   O - kie   from   Mus - ko - gee;

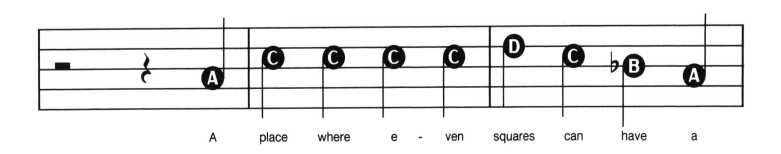

A   place   where   e - ven   squares   can   have   a

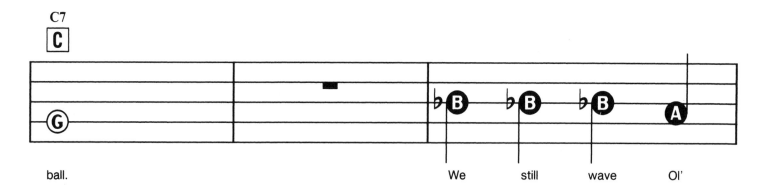

ball.   We   still   wave   Ol'

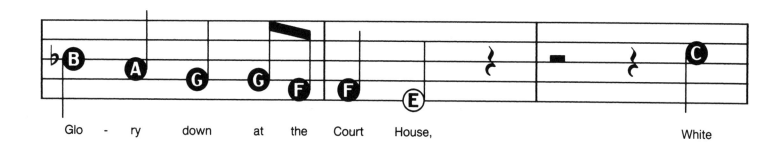

Glo - ry   down   at   the   Court   House,   White

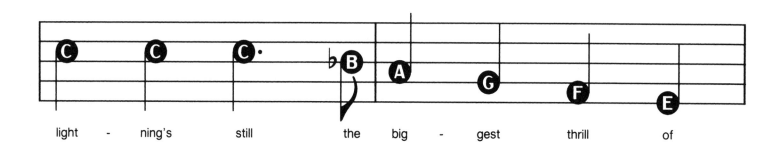

light - ning's   still   the   big - gest   thrill   of

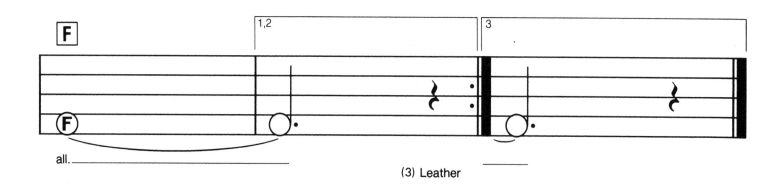

all._____

(3) Leather

Ramblin' Man

Registration 3
Rhythm: Country Western or Swing

Words and Music by
Hank Williams

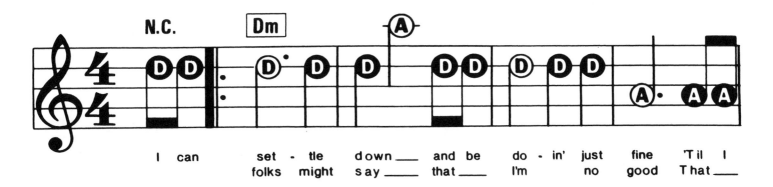

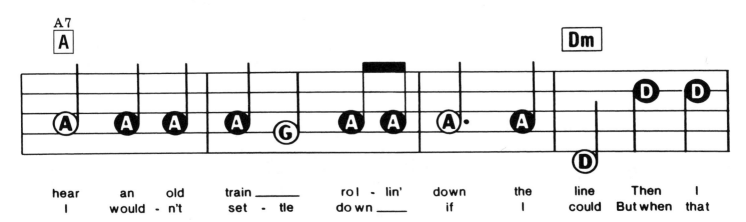

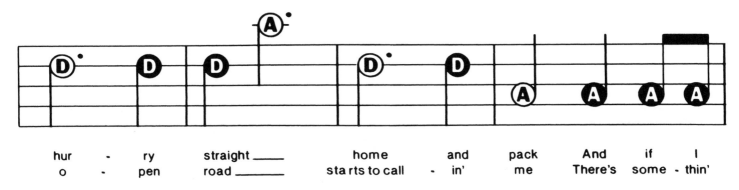

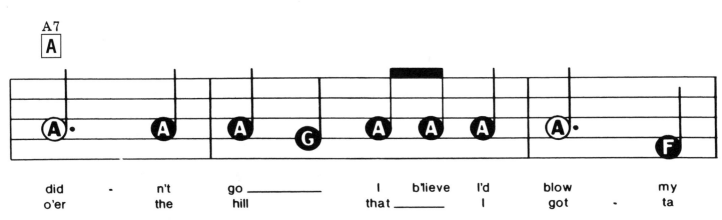

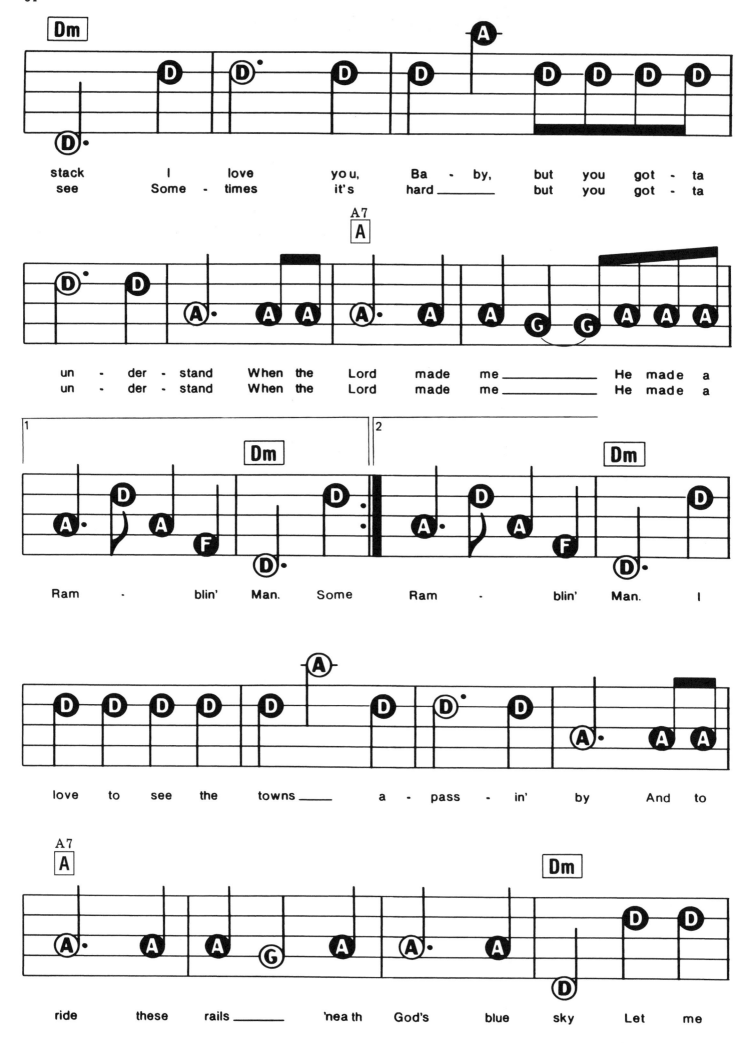

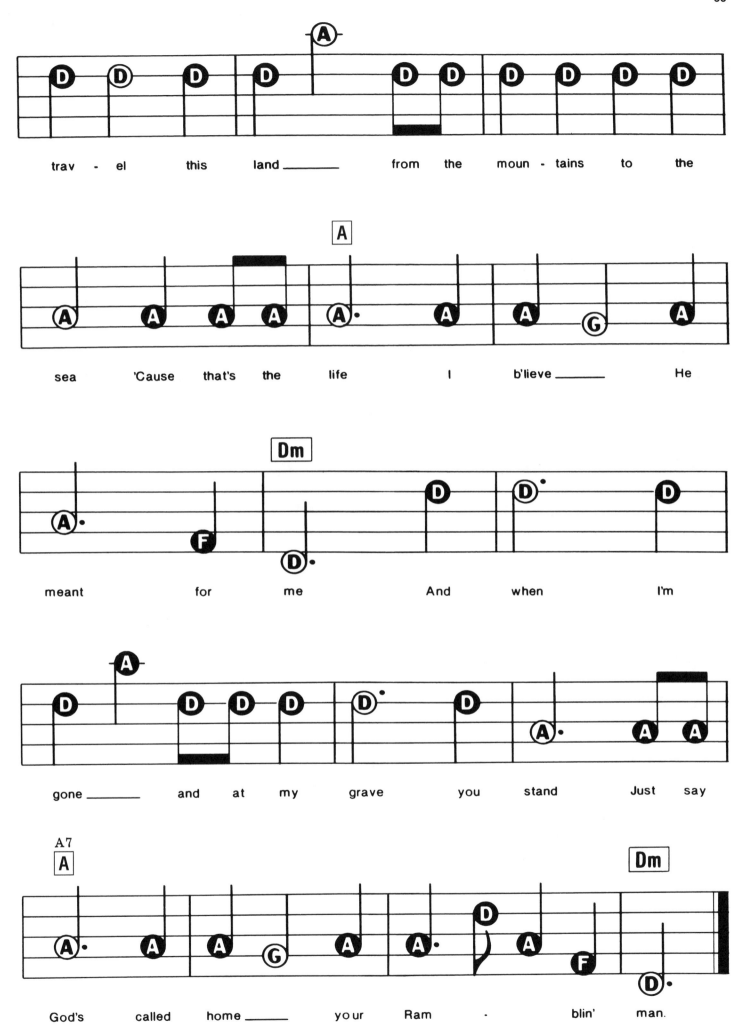

Oye Como Va

Registration 8
Rhythm: Latin Rock or Bossa Nova

Words and Music by
Tito Puente

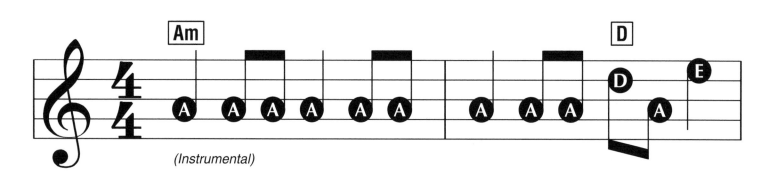

(Instrumental)

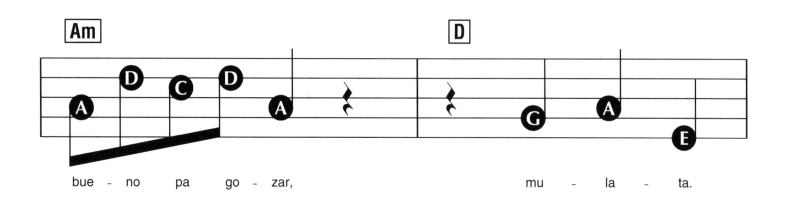

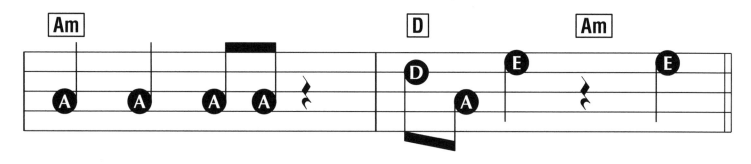

O - ye co - mo va,   mi rit - mo,

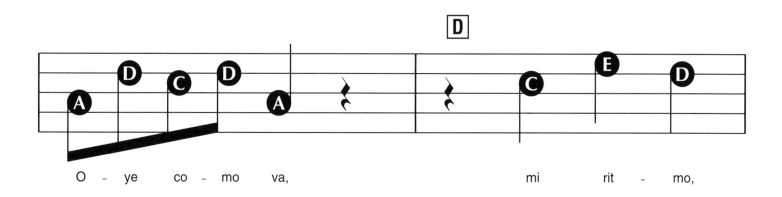

bue - no pa go - zar,   mu - la - ta.

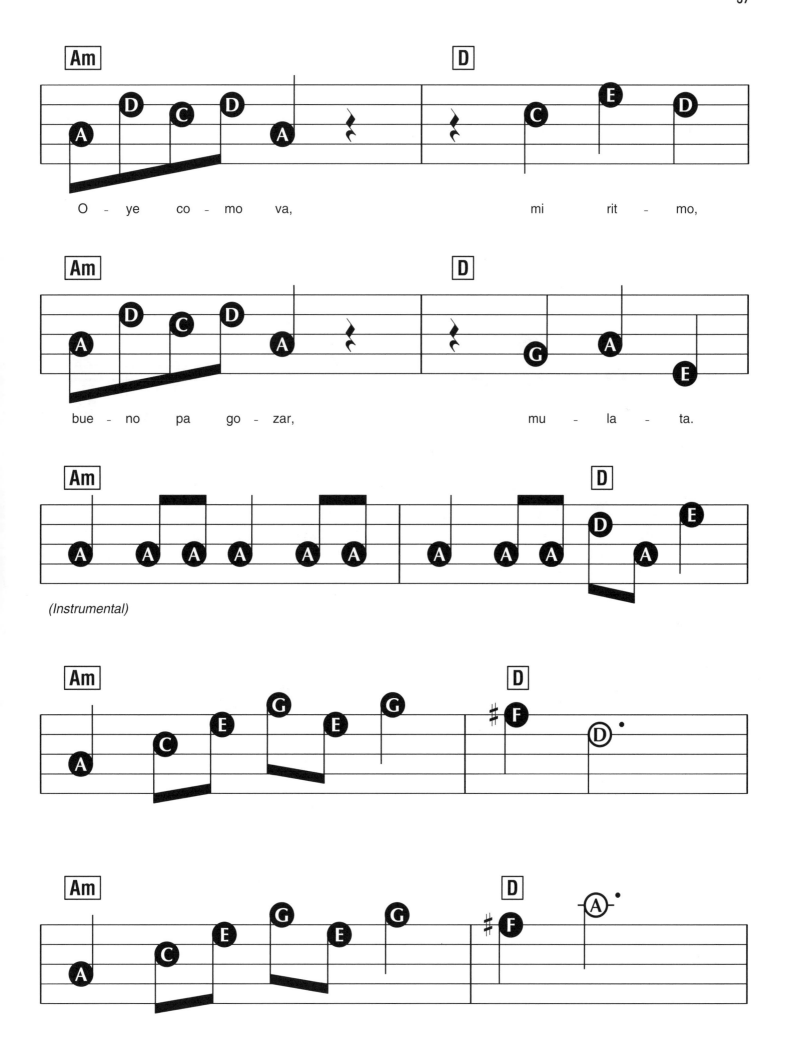

O – ye co – mo va, mi rit – mo,

bue – no pa go – zar, mu – la – ta.

(Instrumental)

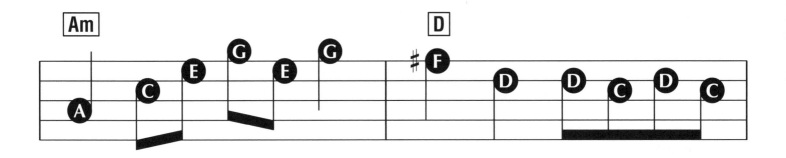

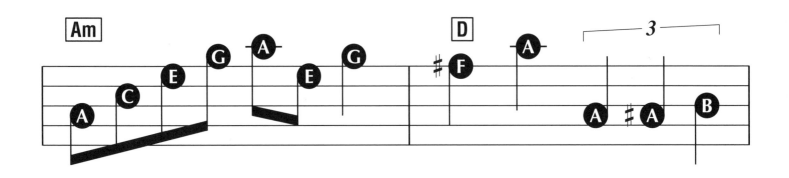

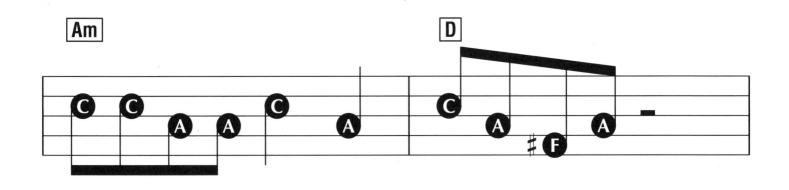

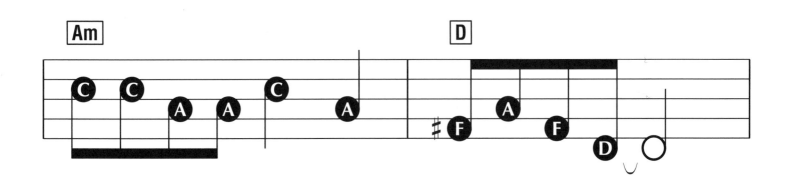

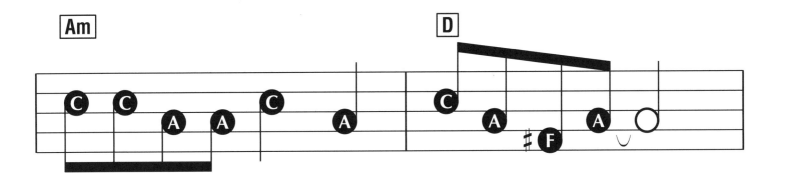

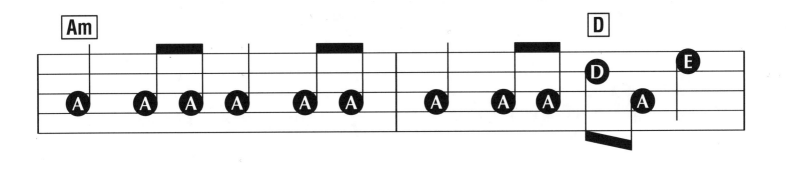

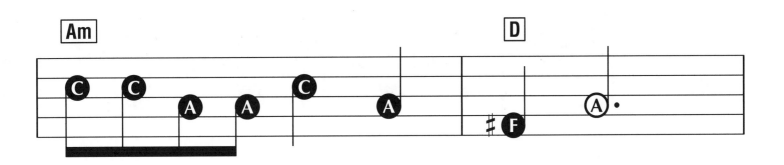

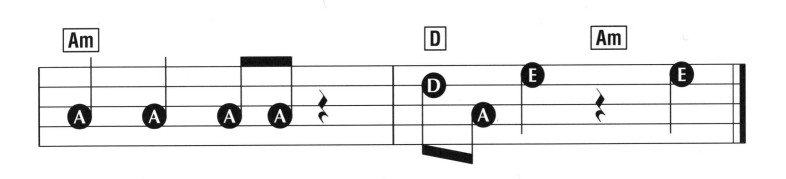

Paperback Writer

Registration 4
Rhythm: Rock

Words and Music by John Lennon
and Paul McCartney

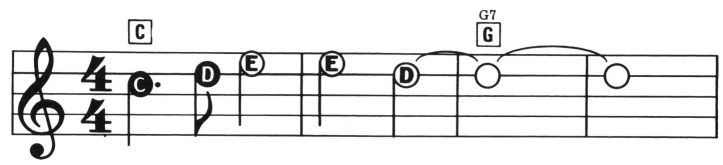

Pa - per - back writ - er. _____

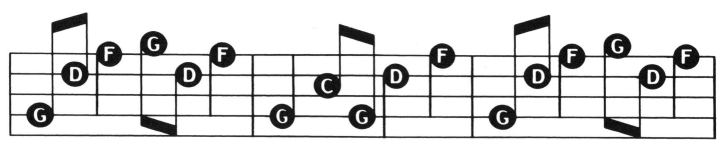

(Instrumental)

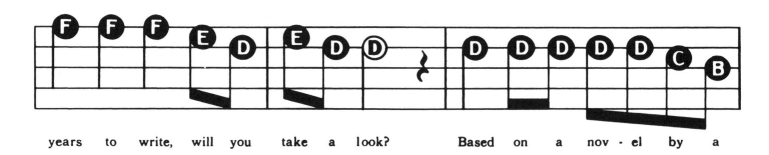

Dear ___ Sir or Ma - dam will you read my book? It took me

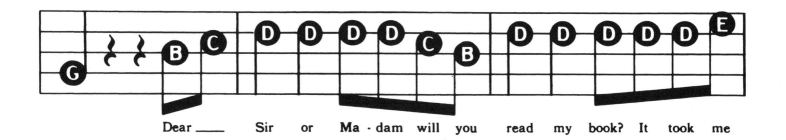

years to write, will you take a look? Based on a nov - el by a

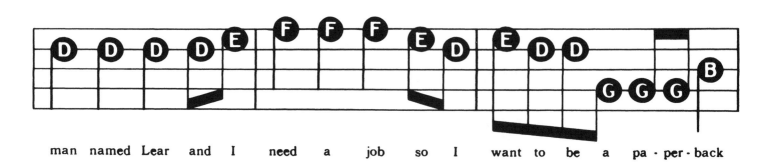

man named Lear and I need a job so I want to be a pa - per - back

61

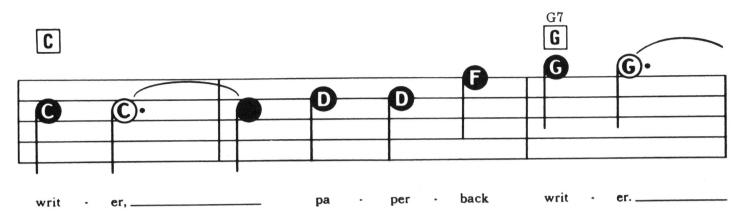

writ - er, _____ pa - per - back writ - er. _____

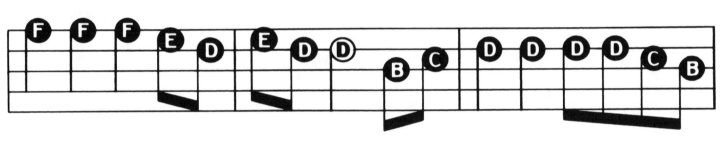

_____ It's the dirt - y sto - ry of a dirt - y man, and his

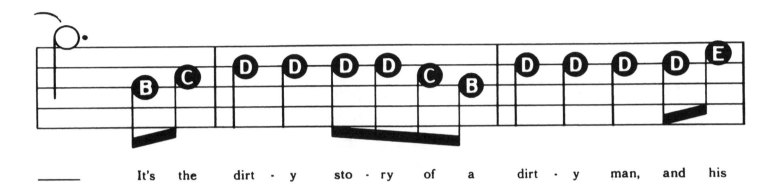

cling - ing wife does - n't un - der - sta nd. His son is work - ing for the

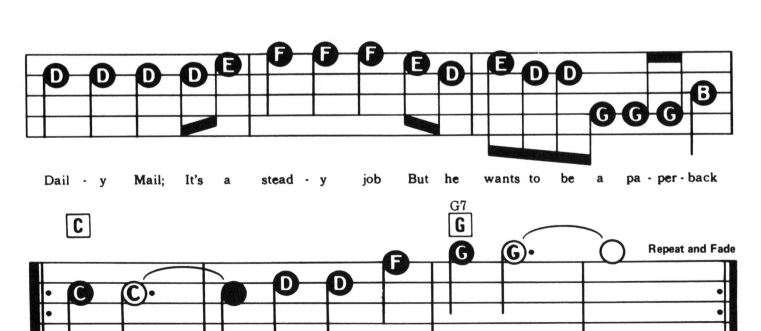

Dail - y Mail; It's a stead - y job But he wants to be a pa - per - back

writ - er. _____ pa - per - back writ - er. _____

Pistol Packin' Mama

Registration 9
Rhythm: Polka, Country or Fox Trot

Words and Music by
Al Dexter

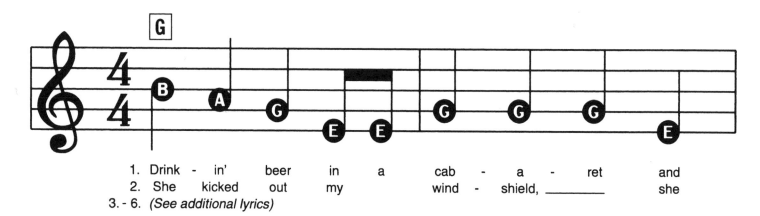

1. Drink - in' beer in a cab - a - ret and
2. She kicked out my wind - shield, _____ she
3. - 6. (See additional lyrics)

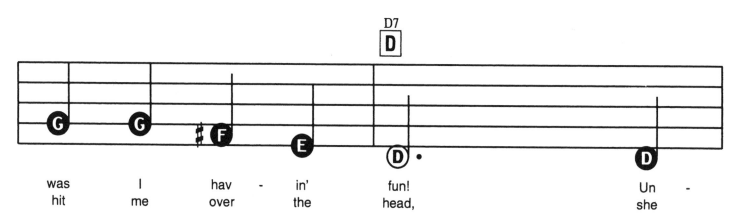

was   I   hav - in'   fun!   Un -
hit   me   over   the   head,   she

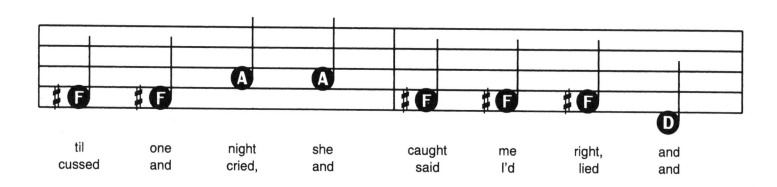

til   one   night   she   caught   me   right,   and
cussed   and   cried,   she   and   said   I'd   lied   and

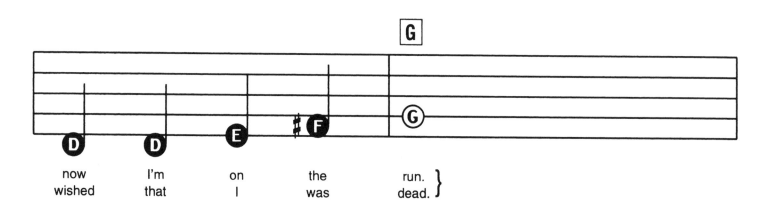

now   I'm   on   the   run. }
wished   that   I   was   dead. }

Chorus

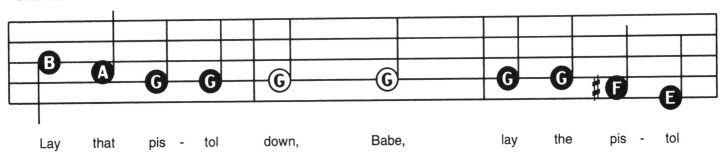

Lay that pis - tol down, Babe, lay the pis - tol

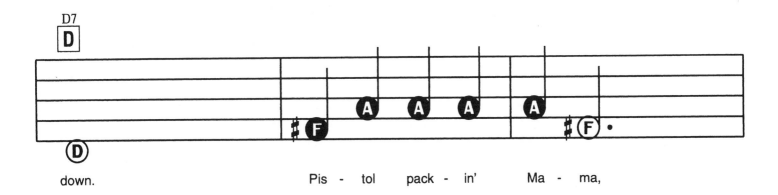

down. Pis - tol pack - in' Ma - ma,

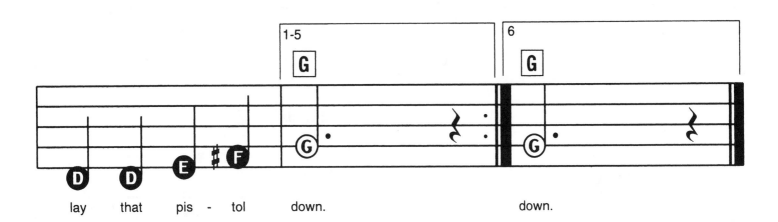

lay that pis - tol down. down.

Additional Lyrics

3. Drinkin' beer in a cabaret, and dancing with a blonde,
Until one night she shot out the light. Bang! That blonde was gone.
Chorus

4. See you ev'ry night, Babe, I'll woo you ev'ry day,
I'll be your regular Daddy, if you'll put that gun away.
Chorus

5. Drinkin' beer in a cabaret, and was I havin' fun!
Until one night she caught me right, and now I'm on the run.
Chorus

6. There was old Al Dexter, he always had his fun.
But with some lead, she shot him dead; his honkin' days are done.
Chorus

Rainy Day Woman

Registration 4
Rhythm: Country

Words and Music by
Waylon Jennings

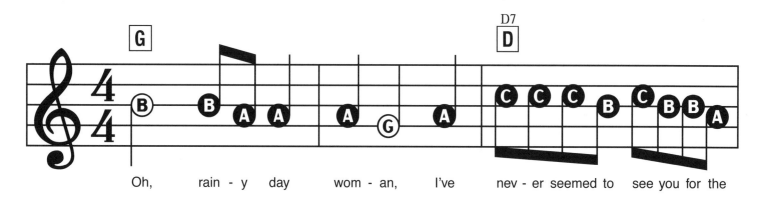

Oh, rain - y day wom - an, I've nev - er seemed to see you for the

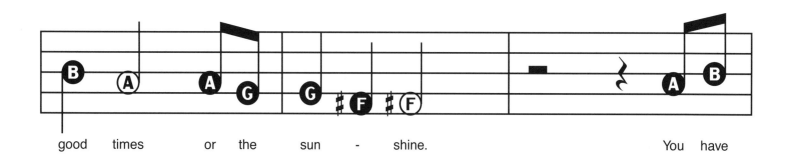

good times or the sun - shine. You have

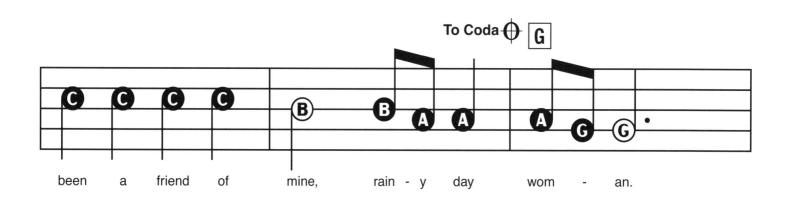

been a friend of mine, rain - y day wom - an.

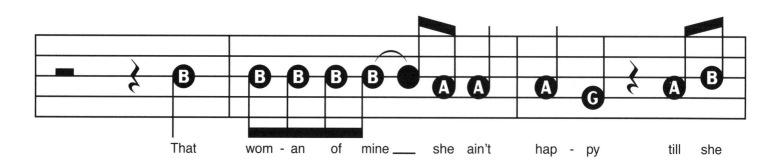

That wom - an of mine ___ she ain't hap - py till she

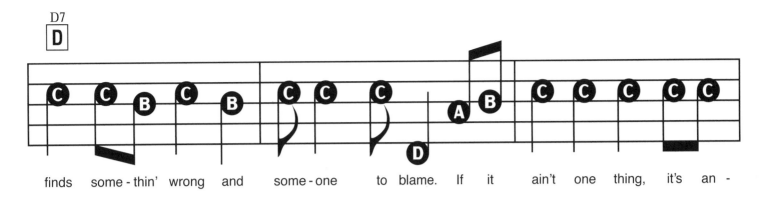

finds some-thin' wrong and some-one to blame. If it ain't one thing, it's an-

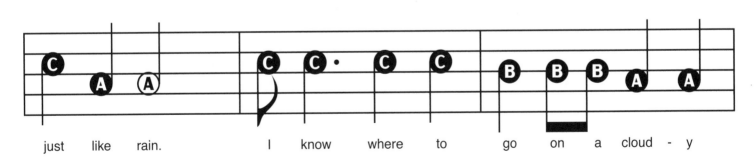

oth-er one on _____ the way.

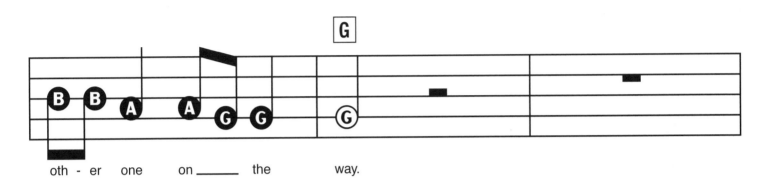

Woke up this morn-in' to the sun - shine. Sure as hell, looks

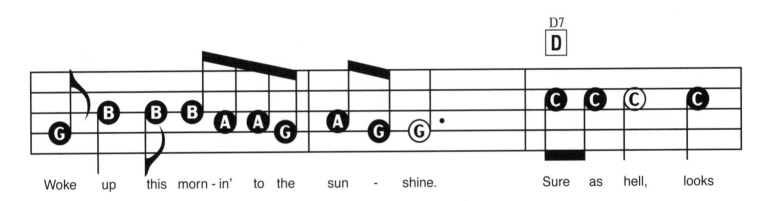

just like rain. I know where to go on a cloud-y

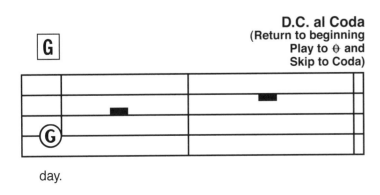

day.

D.C. al Coda
(Return to beginning
Play to ⊕ and
Skip to Coda)

CODA

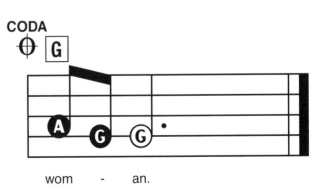

wom - an.

Respect Yourself

Registration 8
Rhythm: 8-Beat or Soul

Words and Music by Mack Rice
and Luther Ingram

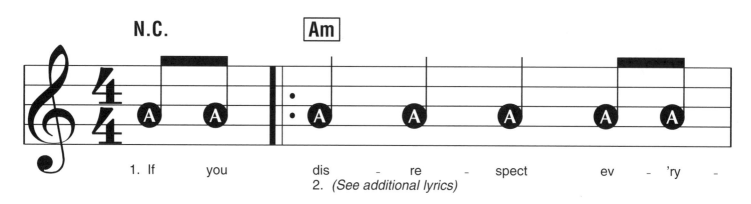

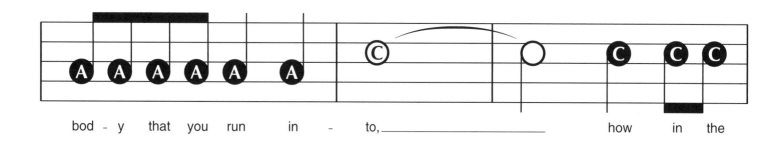

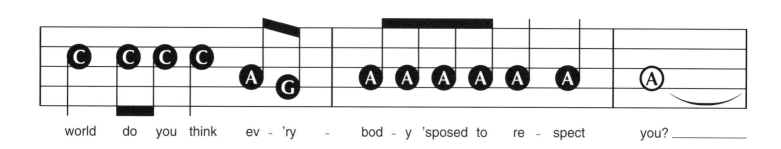

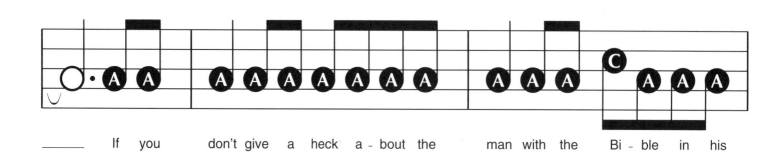

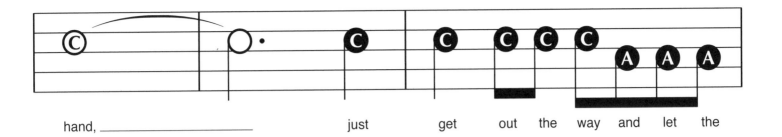

hand, _____ _____ just get out the way and let the

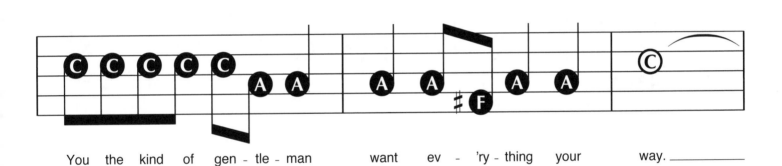

gen – tle – man do his thing. _____

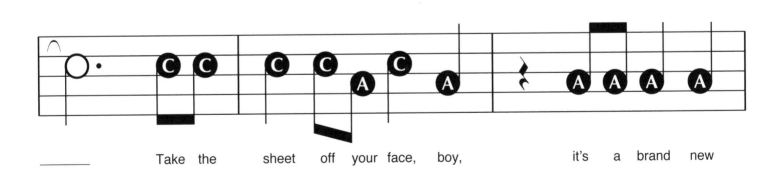

You the kind of gen – tle – man want ev – 'ry – thing your way. _____

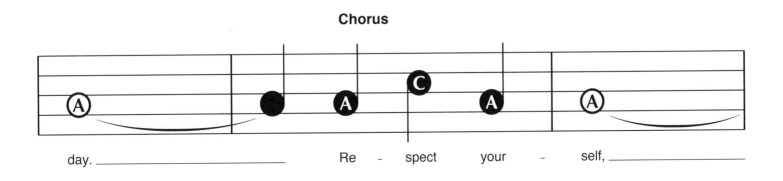

_____ Take the sheet off your face, boy, it's a brand new

Chorus

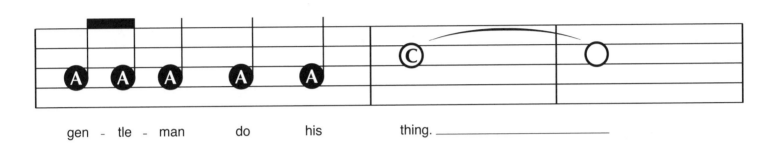

day. _____ Re – spect your – self, _____

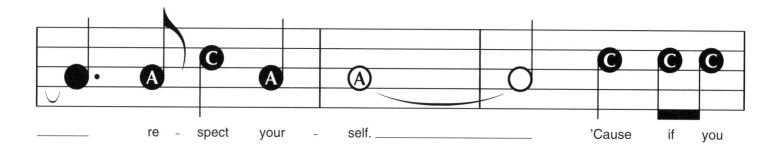

_____ re - spect your - self. _____ 'Cause if you

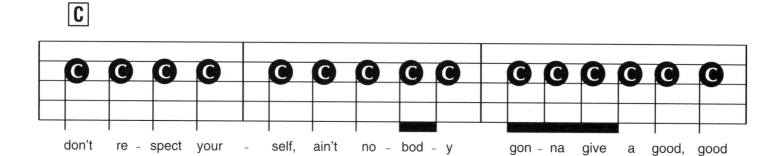

don't re - spect your - self, ain't no - bod - y gon - na give a good, good

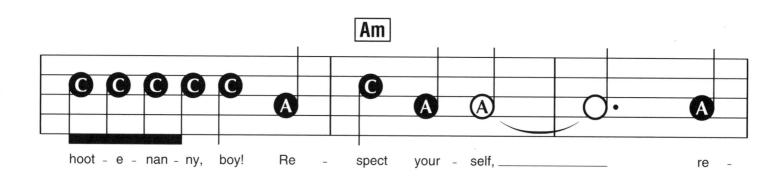

hoot - e - nan - ny, boy! Re - spect your - self, _____ re -

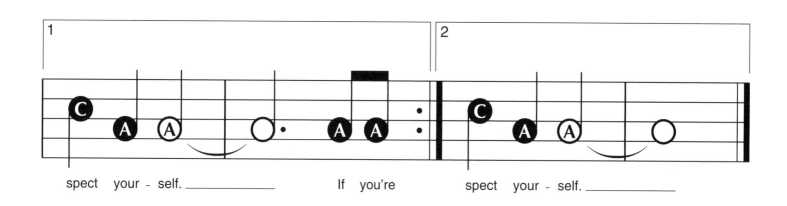

spect your - self. _____ If you're   spect your - self. _____

Additional Lyrics

2. If you're walking around thinking that the world
   Owes you something 'cause you're here,
   You're going out the world backward like you did
   When you first came 'ere.
   Keep talking about the president won't stop air pollution.
   Put your hand over your mouth when you cough; that'll help the solution.
   You cuss around women folk, don't even know their name,
   Then you're dumb enough to think it makes you a big ole man.
   Chorus

That's the Way
(I Like It)

Registration 7
Rhythm: Funk or Rock

Words and Music by Harry Wayne Casey
and Richard Finch

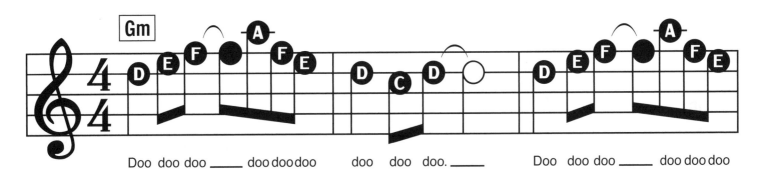

Doo doo doo ____ doo doo doo   doo   doo   doo. ____   Doo doo doo ____ doo doo doo

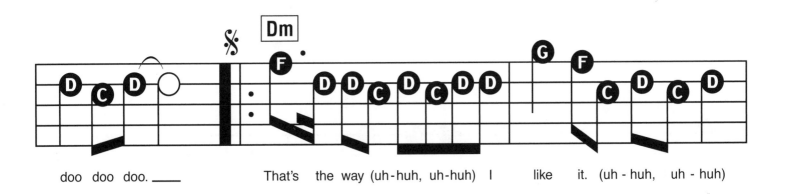

doo doo doo. ____   That's   the way (uh-huh, uh-huh) I   like it. (uh-huh,   uh-huh)

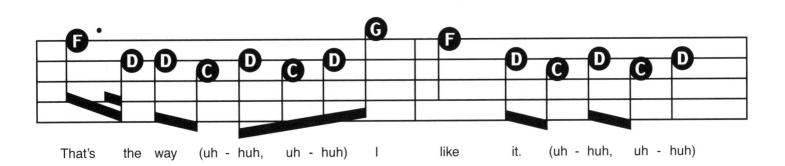

That's   the   way (uh-huh, uh-huh)   I   like   it. (uh-huh, uh-huh)

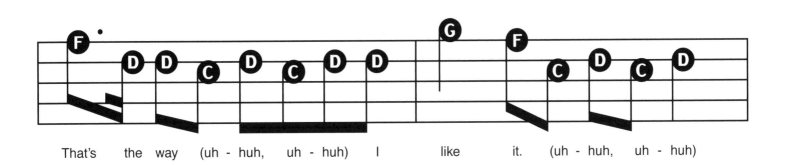

That's   the   way (uh-huh, uh-huh) I   like   it. (uh-huh, uh-huh)

To Coda

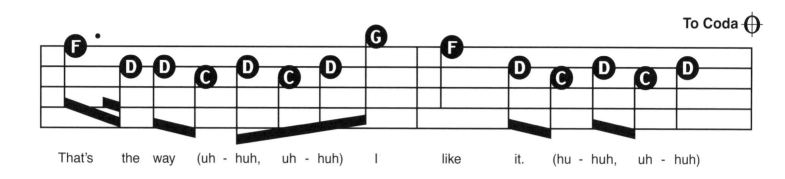

That's   the   way   (uh - huh,   uh - huh)   I   like   it.   (hu - huh,   uh - huh)

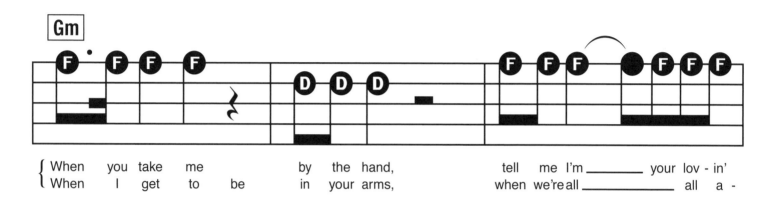

When   you   take   me   by   the   hand,   tell   me   I'm _____ your   lov - in'
When   I   get   to   be   in   your   arms,   when   we're all _____ all   a -

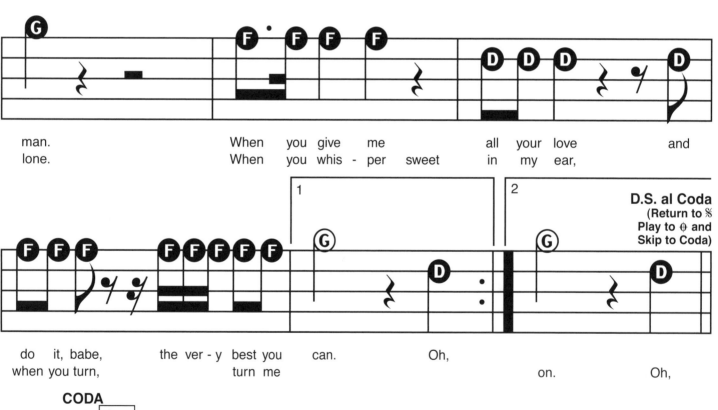

man.   When   you   give   me   all   your   love   and
lone.   When   you   whis - per   sweet   in   my   ear,

D.S. al Coda
(Return to %
Play to ⊕ and
Skip to Coda)

do   it,   babe,   the   ver - y   best   you   can.   Oh,
when   you   turn,   turn   me   on.   Oh,

CODA

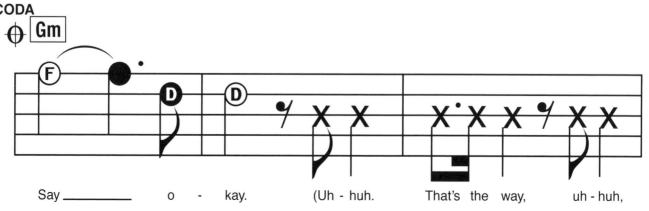

Say _____ o - kay.   (Uh - huh.   That's   the   way,   uh - huh,

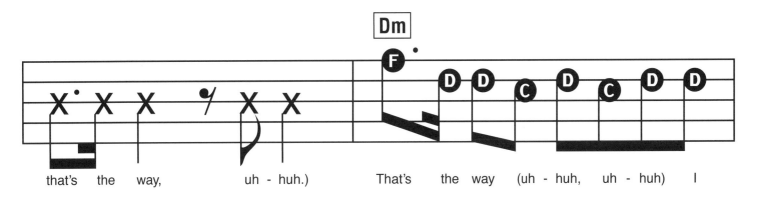

that's the way, uh - huh.) That's the way (uh - huh, uh - huh) I

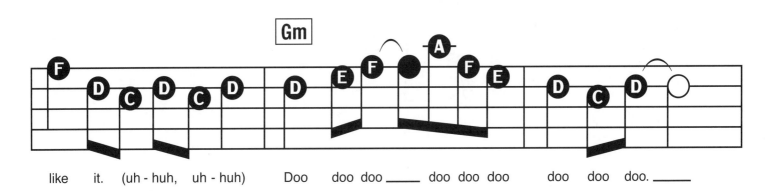

like it. (uh - huh, uh - huh) That's the way (uh - huh, uh - huh) I

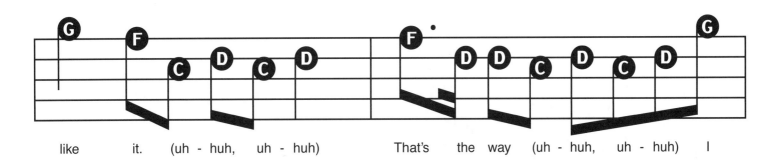

like it. (uh - huh, uh - huh) Doo doo doo _____ doo doo doo doo doo doo. _____

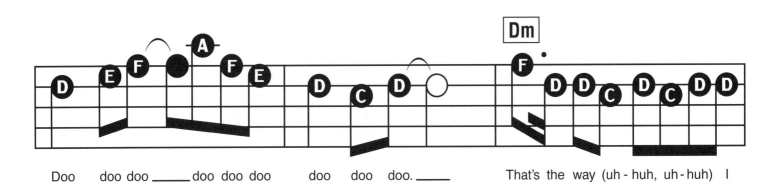

Doo doo doo _____ doo doo doo doo doo doo. _____ That's the way (uh - huh, uh - huh) I

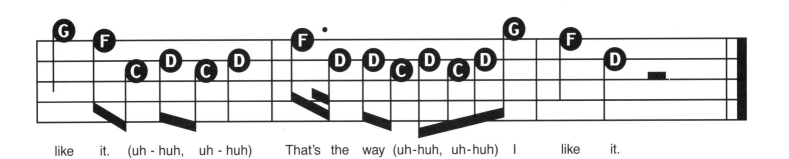

like it. (uh - huh, uh - huh) That's the way (uh-huh, uh-huh) I like it.

Tomorrow Never Knows

Registration 4
Rhythm: 8-Beat or Rock

Words and Music by John Lennon
and Paul McCartney

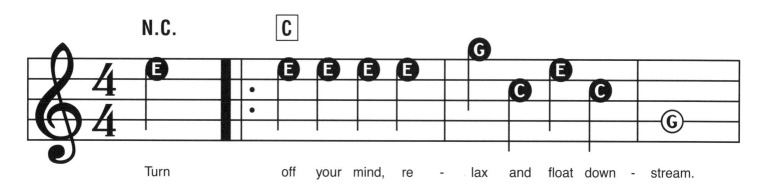

Turn off your mind, re - lax and float down - stream.

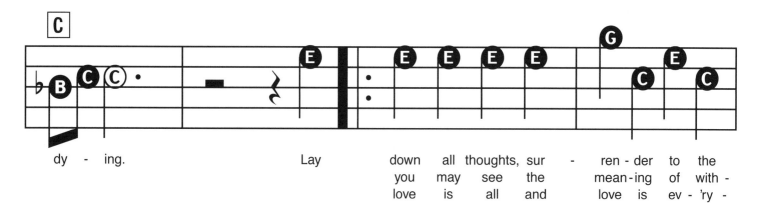

It is not dy - ing. It is not

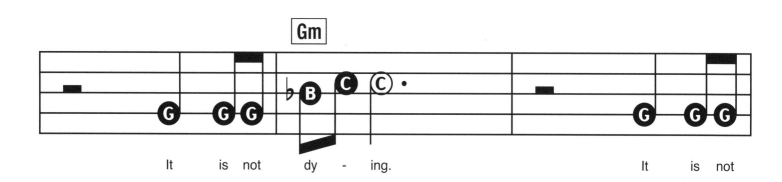

dy - ing. Lay down all thoughts, sur - ren - der to the
you may see the mean - ing of with -
love is all and love is ev - 'ry -

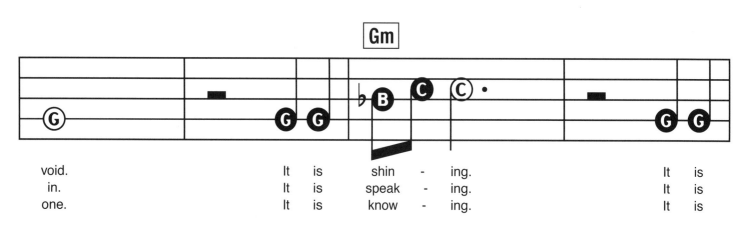

void. It is shin - ing. It is
in. It is speak - ing. It is
one. It is know - ing. It is

Waltz Across Texas

Registration 3
Rhythm: Waltz

Words and Music by
Talmadge Tubb

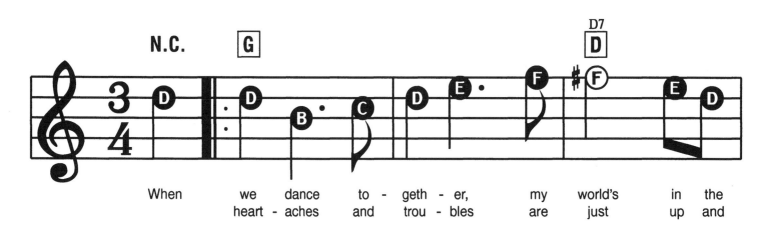

When we dance to - geth - er, my world's in the
heart - aches and trou - bles are just up and

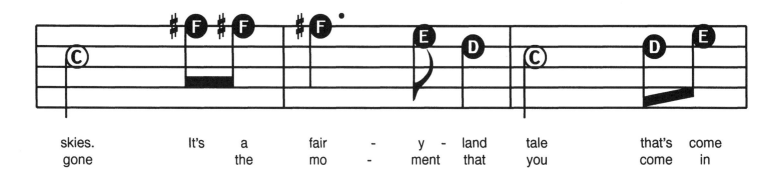

skies. It's a fair - y - land tale that's come
gone the mo - ment that you come in

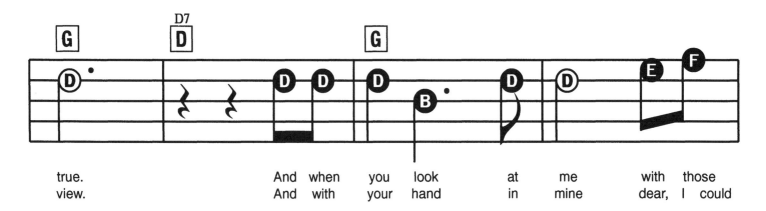

true. And when you look at me with those
view. And with your hand in mine dear, I could

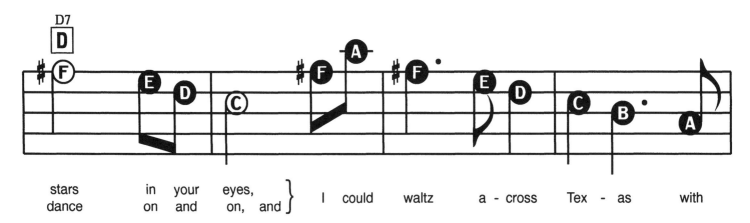

stars in your eyes, } I could waltz a - cross Tex - as with
dance on and on, and

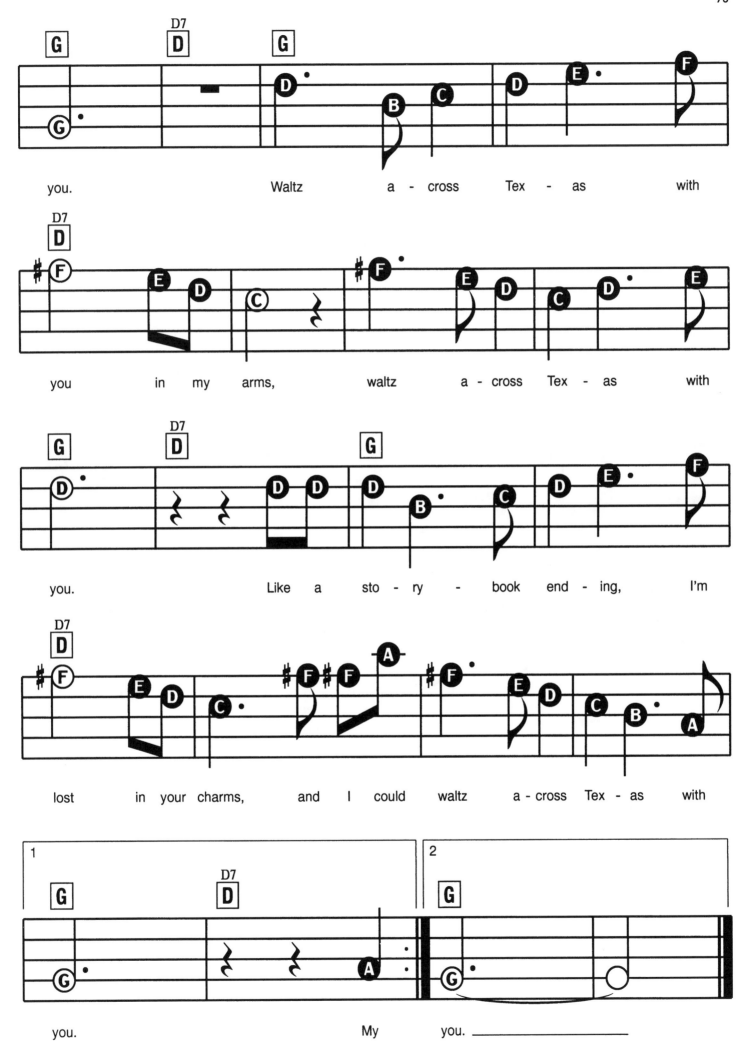

you.   Waltz   a - cross   Tex - as   with

you   in   my   arms,   waltz   a - cross   Tex - as   with

you.   Like   a   sto - ry - book   end - ing,   I'm

lost   in   your   charms,   and   I   could   waltz   a - cross   Tex - as   with

you.   My   you. _____

Tulsa Time

Registration 7
Rhythm: Rock

Words and Music by
Danny Flowers

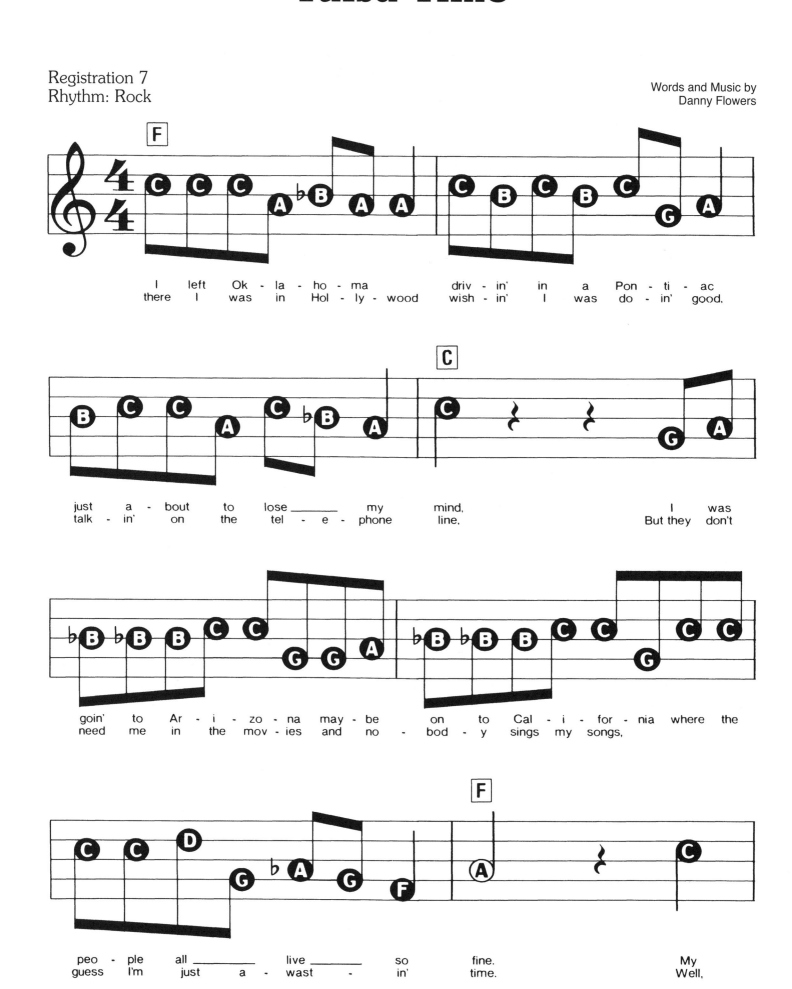

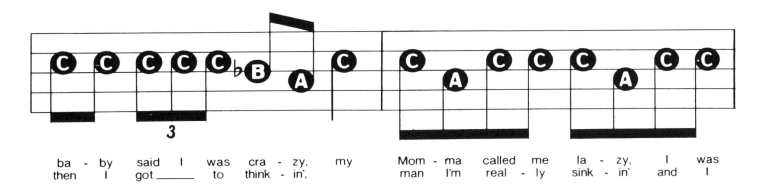

ba - by said I was cra - zy, my Mom - ma called me la - zy, I was
then I got _____ to think - in', man I'm real - ly sink - in' and I

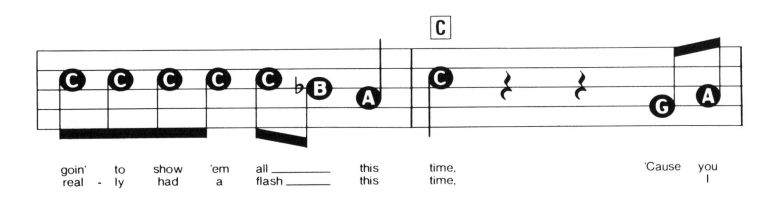

goin' to show 'em all _____ this time, 'Cause you
real - ly had a flash _____ this time, I

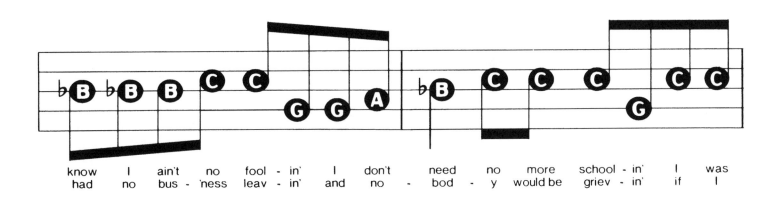

know I ain't no fool - in' I don't need no more school - in' I was
had no bus - 'ness leav - in' and no - bod - y would be griev - in' if I

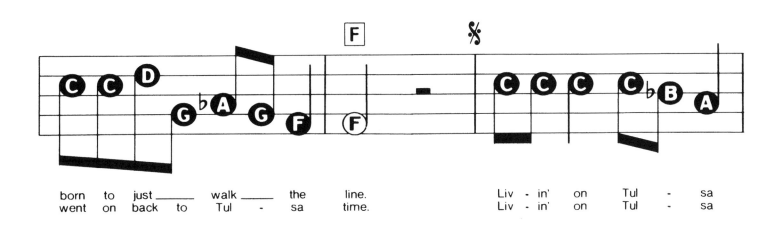

born to just _____ walk _____ the line. Liv - in' on Tul - sa
went on back to Tul - sa time. Liv - in' on Tul - sa

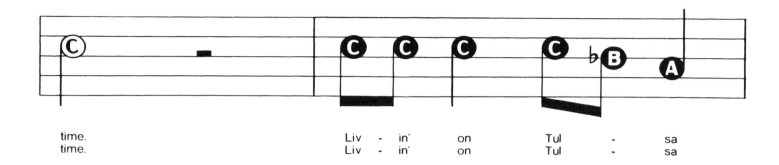

time.
time.

Liv - in' on Tul - sa
Liv - in' on Tul - sa

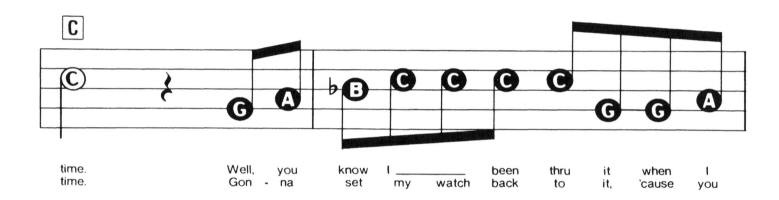

time.
time.

Well, you know I _____ been thru it when I
Gon - na set my watch back to it, 'cause you

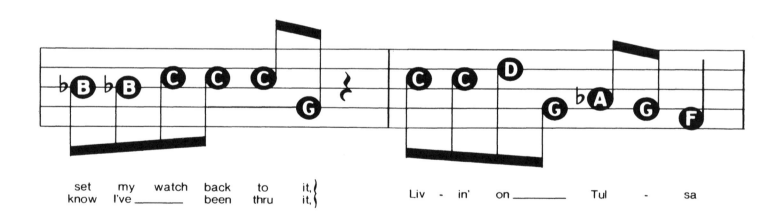

set my watch back to it,
know I've _____ been thru it,

Liv - in' on _____ Tul - sa

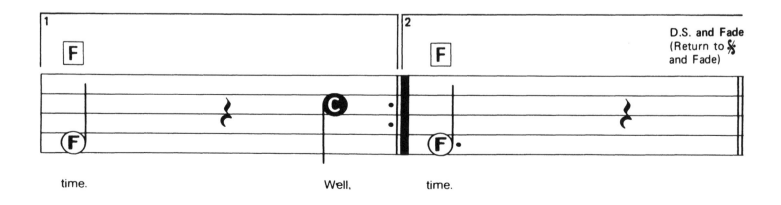

time.

Well, time.

Registration Guide

- Match the Registration number on the song to the corresponding numbered category below. Select and activate an instrumental sound available on your instrument.

- Choose an automatic rhythm appropriate to the mood and style of the song. (Consult your Owner's Guide for proper operation of automatic rhythm features.)

- Adjust the tempo and volume controls to comfortable settings.

Registration

1	Mellow	Flutes, Clarinet, Oboe, Flugel Horn, Trombone, French Horn, Organ Flutes
2	Ensemble	Brass Section, Sax Section, Wind Ensemble, Full Organ, Theater Organ
3	Strings	Violin, Viola, Cello, Fiddle, String Ensemble, Pizzicato, Organ Strings
4	Guitars	Acoustic/Electric Guitars, Banjo, Mandolin, Dulcimer, Ukulele, Hawaiian Guitar
5	Mallets	Vibraphone, Marimba, Xylophone, Steel Drums, Bells, Celesta, Chimes
6	Liturgical	Pipe Organ, Hand Bells, Vocal Ensemble, Choir, Organ Flutes
7	Bright	Saxophones, Trumpet, Mute Trumpet, Synth Leads, Jazz/Gospel Organs
8	Piano	Piano, Electric Piano, Honky Tonk Piano, Harpsichord, Clavi
9	Novelty	Melodic Percussion, Wah Trumpet, Synth, Whistle, Kazoo, Perc. Organ
10	Bellows	Accordion, French Accordion, Mussette, Harmonica, Pump Organ, Bagpipes